ENOUGH SILENCE

Enough Silence

*Creating Sacred Space for Survivors of Sexual Assault
through Restorative Justice*

Cheryl Miller

WILLIAM B. EERDMANS PUBLISHING COMPANY
GRAND RAPIDS, MICHIGAN

Wm. B. Eerdmans Publishing Co.
4035 Park East Court SE, Grand Rapids, Michigan 49546
www.eerdmans.com

Book design by Leah Luyk

Printed in the United States of America

30 29 28 27 26 25 24   1 2 3 4 5 6 7

ISBN 978-0-8028-8371-1

Library of Congress Cataloging-in-Publication Data

A catalog record for this book is available from the Library of
Congress.

Unless otherwise noted, Scripture quotations are from the New Inter-
national Version of the Bible (NIV).

This book is dedicated to the victims and survivors of sexual violence who still endure suffering, who understand the yearning for justice, and who continually search for healing and hope. You are not forgotten and you are heard.

CONTENTS

PREFACE

"It was as if a boulder has been sitting on my chest for the last ten years, slowly crushing the breath out of me, crushing the life out of me, and now it's gone." Those were the words of a survivor after a two-hour mediated session with the man who committed the crime against her. According to her statement, ten years of slowly suffocating, slowly dying is gone in just two short hours. She said, "Now, it's as if I can breathe again, live again." Powerful words to describe a powerful process.

I volunteer as a mediator for a victim-offender dialogue program and have done mediations for over twenty years between victims of violent crime and their offenders. The session described above was one of the first mediations I did, and when I heard the words "Now, it's as if I can breathe again, live again," I knew I was a part of something powerful and sacred. That mediation set me on a journey to understand why and how such a dramatic transformation occurred in such a short time. As a result, I have also realized that restorative justice processes like victim-offender dialogue or circles can help survivors of sexual violence.

As you read through the first-hand accounts of this process, what I hope will emerge are new opportunities from new ideas that challenge you to be the one who says, *enough silence*. It is time to speak and listen and create systems and programs that bring healing and begin the process of dismantling paternalistic structures that allow women to be treated less than, that allow women to suffer harassment in the workplace and our churches, that create spaces where women, men, and little girls and boys are subject to horrors of sexual violence.

I would like to express my deep gratitude to my dear friends Judith Williams and Annette Yancey who encouraged me and prayed for years that one day this book and this story would become a reality. God heard your prayers. I would also like to express much appreciation to Keely Boeving, my agent, for her belief this was a story that needed to be told and her incredible support and encouragement during some of the dark nights of the writing. And finally, Lisa Ann Cockrel, my editor, who believed that Cheryl Miller from a small town, in the middle of nowhere, might have something to say. Words cannot express the gratitude for all you did to shape this book and story into what it has become.

INTRODUCTION

Jim Collins introduced the concept of the Big Hairy Audacious Goal—BHAG for short—in his book *Built to Last*. But we live in a society of Big, Hairy Audacious Problems. Sexual violence is one of the most damaging problems in society—and it is prevalent in our offices, churches, neighborhoods, and homes. Unfortunately, our societal institutions—including the church—have failed survivors miserably. Often survivors are dismissed, ignored, or overlooked. We have done a horrible job of expecting accountability from the perpetrator by looking the other way, failing to report, and allowing toxic paternalistic environments where predators are free to groom and assault. But that can change.

Important Warnings

- The content of this book may be difficult for some readers and may cause triggers for those who have suffered from sexual violence. Each chapter begins with the story of a woman survivor of child sexual assault. The sections with her story are emotional and difficult. If you are a survivor, know you may experience triggers or unpleasant reactions. Please continue with care.
- Confidentiality is critical in the restorative justice process. Victims must trust that the specific details and dialogue shared in

mediations will remain confidential. So, in order to both teach others about the transformational capacity of this process and also preserve confidentiality, people in this book are fictionalized composite characters I have drawn based on twenty years of experience working with the victims of violent crime.

- All restorative justice processes center around dialogue. While this book will provide insight into the restorative justice process, it will not prepare the reader to be a facilitator of those processes. Instead, this book will provide insights into how restorative justice works, how it impacts those involved, and how it might be used in churches, organizations, and the workplace to address sexual violence. It is my hope that this book will inspire readers to recognize the power of these processes and seek training to become qualified facilitators—the more challenging the issues to be addressed through dialogue, the more training required. Many victim-offender dialogue programs require forty hours of training. Attempting to facilitate a restorative justice process without proper training has potential to cause great harm and re-victimize survivors.

Clara

To better understand the restorative justice tools and processes that all of us can learn and implement, we will follow the story of Clara. As stated above, Clara is a fictional character and the details don't include any particular mediation. Her story is based on a compilation of survivors I have worked with over the past twenty years and accurately reflects survivors' emotions, experiences, and transformation. In this book, Clara is a victim of child sexual assault by her father.

Her father died when she was a young woman, and he was never held accountable nor did he ever acknowledge his crime. Years later, Clara attended a restorative justice conference and was caught off guard when she heard a man named Thomas speak about the crime he committed against his own daughter, an offense similar to the one Clara experienced. That meeting catapulted Clara into a gut-wrenching process of surrogate mediation through a program called Making It Right, a fictional program based on multiple restorative justice models.

Making It Right is a program for sex offenders to take responsibility for their actions with the specific individual they harmed. But they also volunteer to answer questions through mediated dialogue with other victims of sexual assault whose offenders were never convicted or took responsibility for the harm to their victim. The Making It Right program allows victims like Clara to participate in a surrogate mediation. Surrogate mediation is a voluntary process where an offender is willing to sit in the seat of the victim's actual offender and answer questions as someone who harmed another person. What makes this process even more intriguing is the willingness of a stranger to sit in the place of someone else who injured another greatly and face the person they hurt. It is a gift and a recompense, and both are offered freely.

The surrogate process differs from a victim-offender dialogue between the actual victim and offender. However, it is still transformative, as you will discover through Clara's and Thomas's stories. We will follow Clara's journey toward the surrogate mediation process as she shows up at the beginning of each chapter and recounts parts of her journey over the months it took to prepare for a mediated dialogue. Each part of Clara's story highlights the concepts or tools that make the process so transformative and impactful. We learn from Clara that even those we deem our greatest enemy can be offered grace and love.

Clara's story can be hard to read. She has been silenced in multiple spaces over the years because of the discomfort of others: family who did not want to relive what Clara experienced daily; friends who grew weary of hearing her talk about her pain; church members who were gossiping about sin or demanding she forgive. And for a while, she silenced herself, carrying the pain alone. Eventually, she realized healing would come by talking about and sharing her journey. This poem by another survivor—shared here with permission—reflects the power of the story and the realization that came when she said, enough silence!

> Look at me.
> Do you see me?
> Beneath my skin are jagged scars,
> pink wounds barely healed.
>
> The story of those wounds is ugly
> but you need to look,
> to listen, and see me.
>
> I walked through the death
> and yet emerged alive.
> Look at me.
>
> I didn't die.
> I didn't die.
> What I survived is ugly and
> I wanted to die, but I didn't.
>
> My story, twisted and
> ugly, must be told
> because
>
> my journey of wading through filth
> and trails of blood
> did not end in death.
> The destination was power and truth.

I cannot be silent.
In telling, I reveal I survived.

And I am not ugly.
I am beautiful.

Sexual Violence

For the purposes of this book, sexual violence refers to the span of harm that is done sexually to an individual. The forms of sexual violence are wide, including rape/murder, rape, sexual assault, intimate partner violence, child sexual abuse, incest, stalking, sexual harassment and discrimination based on gender or sexual identity. Anyone can be the target of sexual violence, which affects people of every age, gender identity, and sexual orientation. RAINN (Rape, Abuse & Incest National Network) provides excellent data on sexual violence in the United States. Ninety percent of rape survivors are women and 10 percent are men; young people are the highest risk for sexual violence at 69 percent (12–17: 15 percent and 18–34: 54 percent).[1]

Some survivors never report their crimes, out of fear—fear of retaliation by the perpetrator, fear of re-victimization, and fear of not being believed. In addition, blaming the victim is common in our society. According to a report from the U.S. Department of Justice, in 2016, only 23 percent of victims of sexual assault or rape reported the crime to the police. That number is down from the previous year in 2015 when 32 percent were reported.[2] According to a research review reported by the National Sexual Violence Resource Center, false reports happen in 2 to 10 percent of cases.[3]

According to the Office for Victims of Crime (OVS), "Statistics documenting transgender people's experience of sexual violence indicate shockingly high levels of sexual abuse and assault. One in two transgender individuals are sexually abused or assaulted at some point in their lives. Some reports estimate that transgender survivors may experience rates of sexual assault up to 66 percent, often coupled with physical assaults or abuse."[4]

The Pew Research Center states that a recent survey "asked LGBT respondents to rate six religions or religious institutions as friendly, neutral or unfriendly toward the LGBT population. By overwhelming margins, most rate all six as more unfriendly than friendly."[5]

We have much to do to address all forms of sexual violence in our homes, communities, workplaces and places of worship and restorative justice is a wonderful place to start. Restorative justice has its roots in the most extreme form of sexual violence with victims of severe violent crimes, like rape/murder, rape, sexual assault, and child sexual assault. The good news is that the principles in this book can address the range of forms of sexual violence where violence is still present but less severe like harassment and discrimination.

Why This Book

#Metoo and #churchtoo have inspired many survivors to take a courageous step and report the crimes committed against them. But there is still much work to do. An alarming 77 percent of victims do not report. Those 77 percent choose to remain invisible and suffer in silence. A woman who participated in a victim-offender mediation ten years after the crime shared how she was sitting in church the following Sunday after meeting with the man who raped her. No one in her church knew she had been raped because she never told anyone due to the judgmental comments and inappropriate responses she had already experienced from friends who were a part of other faith communities. That morning she knew it was time to put that night on the cross. It was time to release the fear. It was a state-funded mediation program that provided healing for the victim and allowed her to release some trauma. What must not be missed is that this woman sat in the pews of her church for ten years, suffering alone. She never told anyone in her church about the crime out of fear they would judge her. After ten years of suffering alone, it is time to stop that offense. It is time to say, enough silence.

It is time for the church to follow the teaching of Christ found in the story of the woman with an issue of blood. In Mark 5:30–34 Jesus was touched, unseen, by the woman.

> At once Jesus realized that power had gone out from him. He turned around in the crowd and asked, "Who touched my clothes?"
>
> "You see the people crowding against you," his disciples answered, "and yet you can ask, 'Who touched me?'"
>
> But Jesus kept looking around to see who had done it. Then the woman, knowing what had happened to her, came and fell at his feet and, trembling with fear, told him the whole truth. He said to her, "Daughter, your faith has healed you. Go in peace and be freed from your suffering."

Note the fact that the woman was unseen. Not just unseen by Jesus but unseen by everyone around her. But Jesus models for us how to respond to the unseen. Jesus stopped and kept looking until he found her. We must be willing to do the same. We must stop and search for the unseen, those who have been silenced and pushed to the margins. Churches and organizations must create a safe place for victims of rape, sexual assault, or harassment to speak out without fear of retaliation, disbelief, or re-victimization. This must be more than lip service of simply wanting to be a safe place, or safer spaces, but taking the steps necessary to provide it.

It is time to follow Christ, to look for those hidden in the shadows of shame and fear, and to offer healing, peace, and freedom from suffering.

There are three sections in this book. The first section will explore the philosophy, elements, concepts, and various processes of restorative justice. The goal is to provide a deep understanding of restorative justice and the value it brings to our communities, organizations, and churches. The first section focuses on the "what" of restorative justice.

The second section explores the individuals impacted by sexual violence, both the survivors and the offenders. The goal is to gain insight into the trauma and pain of survivors and to learn how to engage with them to create sacred space for healing. It is vital to recognize that restorative justice is a victim-centered approach. It is also important to understand criminal and harmful thinking and how to respond in a way that creates healing and future safety for all involved. So, the second section focuses on the "who" of restorative justice.

The third section explores next steps for leaders, pastors, and supervisors to implement principles learned in the first two sections. It will cover both what needs to be implemented to create sacred space and what must be dismantled. The third section is the "how" of restorative justice and the most important. I have had countless conversations with pastors about the issues of sexual violence. The one thing that tends to remain common in all those conversations is the lack of tools and training they have had to address these complex issues. This lack of insight, knowledge, and resources creates a perfect storm that allows the destructive winds of sexual violence to prevail in the very spaces that were intended to be a safe harbor. This lack results in ignoring important signs, minimizing serious allegations, and allowing predators free rein. Many survivors of sexual violence have left the church for these very reasons. It is time to do as Jesus did with the woman with the issue of blood. It is time to see them and provide a sacred space for healing.

Words

A few years back, I had a dream, and in the middle of the dream, God whispered to me, "Cheryl, remember the word *quantum*." When I woke up, I knew the dream meant something. However, I had no idea what quantum meant, so I called my niece, a physics teacher. She explained that quantum is the minimum amount of any physical entity. Over the years, I loved learning more about the principles of physics and the idea of quantum, but I always returned to the most straightforward message of smallness, the minimum amount. Every dialogue, every conversation starts with the smallest single word, so we must learn to choose it wisely.

It may seem like conversations are a small and possibly insignificant place to start, but small can be good. It may also seem like just having a conversation won't change anything. But words can bring new life, like the woman who said she could breathe and live again. Christ used three small words, "Lazarus, come out!" (John 11:43) to call Lazarus forth from the tomb. Words are not the tiny insignificant place to start; words and dialogue are the only place to start.

Throughout the book, I use both the terms *victim* and *survivor*. I also use the terms *offender*, *perpetrator*, and *those who have done harm*. The terms *survivor* and *those who have done harm* are suggested to recognize that people are more than just labels. I often get pushback with using the terms *victim* and *offender/perpetrator*. Those words attach labels and can be connected with shame. As much as that is true, it doesn't dismiss the truth of the words and the reality they reflect. I recently had the opportunity to talk with a woman I don't know in person, but I have admired for years,

Debbie Smith, who is a victim of sexual violence and the founder of H-E-A-R-T (Hope Exists After Rape Trauma).[6] Debbie does a wonderful job in a recent blog describing her journey of coming to terms around the words *victim* and *survivor*. She wrote:

> As I continued in my battle between victim and survivor, I realized that all survivors have to be a victim of something before they can be a survivor. Being a survivor cannot change the fact that I am a rape victim. In fact, I needed to admit and understand my victimization before wanting to move to being a survivor. Being a victim is being the innocent party, having no fault, being blameless in the action that took place. I could not skip this step. For me, it was essential to look at and understand that I was a victim of rape because that gave the tremendous hurt a name and reason for being so prevalent in my life.[7]

Because Debbie bravely shares her story publicly, she has become an excellent resource that is referenced multiple times throughout the following chapters. Her accounts are personal and first-hand experiences of the trauma of sexual violence. Several years back, she met with the man who raped her in a victim-offender dialogue. She is one of the few victims who has spoken publicly about the mediation. Again, her willingness to share becomes an excellent resource into the restorative justice processes, giving us a glimpse into the power of the process.

Similarly it may seem harsh to use the labels *offender* and *perpetrator*, or any label attached to a person who has committed a violent crime like murder or rape. Some push back on attaching a label like *murderer* because a person is more than a crime they committed at one point in life, which is completely true. But there is a place to use the word because, let's face it, it is true. And God does not shy away from that reality; the word *murderer* appears twenty-three times in the Bible and *offender* appears four times.

I have sat across the table from individuals as a representative of the mother of a child they killed; she would call them a *murderer*. In that space, the word fits, as do the words *brother*, *son*, *father* or the many other labels each of us carry. There are places and spaces for each word: *victim, survivor, offender, perpetrator, those who have done harm*.

Throughout the book, we will explore insights into restorative justice concepts and tools that can be implemented to create opportunities for both healing and accountability. These tools and ideas are invaluable for leaders of ministries, nonprofits, and organizations. It is time to challenge leaders to examine and then dismantle existing cultures and systems that perpetuate an environment where sexual violence is prevalent and tolerated. It is time to pull back the curtain, look deep into what should be safer spaces, and dig out the cancerous behaviors and values that create a world where five-year-olds are allowed to be ravaged. It is time to say, enough silence!

PART 1

The What

CHAPTER 1

Searching for Justice

"Remember, you can never tell anyone what we do. This is our special time," he whispered in her ear. The sound of those words repeated over and over never ceased to cause her muscles to spasm and her stomach to clench. Did he notice? Did he feel the sensation of her muscles jumping? Did he sense her fear? She knew the answer. Of course, he did. Even if she desperately wished it wasn't so. Every time she would jerk at hearing those words, he would smile. Every single time he came to her room, he whispered those words before leaving. Did he whisper them because he delighted in knowing her fear was so great it ruled her body? Why did he whisper since no one else lived in their home? Or was he terrified one day she would tell?

Clara never really knew when his late-night visits to her room began, but she distinctly remembered the first time. She guessed she was around five or six. Her room was at the top of the stairs. Her father had a large room at the bottom of the stairs. Clara could hear the mumbling of the TV as he watched late-night shows. She could see the warm glow under the crack in her door.

That first night, she drifted to sleep staring at the amber line under the door. But a strange noise woke her. She looked under her door and saw only darkness. *Her father must be asleep*, she thought. She saw someone move beside her bed and she let out a squeak

15

before a hand clasped over her mouth. She was terrified for one moment, but it washed away when she saw her father's face. When he saw her relax, he took his hand off her mouth.

"Hi, daddy," she smiled.

He didn't say a word as he knelt beside her bed. When he didn't answer, Clara was about to say something, but he put his finger to his mouth, shushed her, and told her to be still. She was so confused, but she did as he said. He stared at her and stroked her hair, and she relaxed. She loved his affection. But after a few moments, his hand lifted her nightgown, touching her in places she didn't like. He got a strange smile as he continued to remove her panties. She wanted his attention but didn't like where his hand rested. Finally, after a few minutes, he shook his head and pulled her panties back on roughly before walking out of her room without a word.

This scene repeated over the next few weeks. But one night, things changed. That night when he came into her room he smelled funny. He smelled the way he did when he drank. This time after he removed her panties, he crawled into bed with her. He started to touch her in a painful way. She had no idea what was happening. She knew only that he was hurting her; the pain was so intense that she thought she was dying. Lying on her back, tears rolled into her ears as her father kept on and on, all the while looking into her blue eyes with that strange smile on his face.

Nighttime rituals changed after that. Every night Clara would watch the light under the door, desperately wanting to fall asleep before the darkness came. If she fell asleep first, in her mind, she would be safe. If the light went out, terror would grip her throat, and she would lie stiff, waiting for the monster to come. Looking back as an adult, she realized it didn't matter if she fell asleep first or not. He came anyway. But it allowed her that moment of peace, and she hoped she might be spared. But night after night, he came. Night after night, he hurt her the same way whispering the same words each time: "Remember, you can never tell anyone what we do. This is our special time."

Worse than the words were his eyes. If only he wouldn't look at her. His gaze seemed to penetrate past her big blue eyes and see straight into her soul. If she closed her eyes, he would get angry, and things would be much worse. She learned early on how to stare into the face of a monster and be eaten by shame.

Just as Clara never really knew when his visits started, she also didn't remember exactly when they stopped. She was in junior high when she realized he had not come into her room at night for weeks. That realization filled her with several emotions, hope that maybe, just maybe, it was over. And dread that he was torturing her with a hiatus only to be awakened to the nightmares again. But he never came back. She was ashamed to admit that it made her sad, that she wasn't good enough. Did he no longer want her? Was she ugly?

They were not a typical family. It was just Clara and her father. When Clara was three, her mother was arrested for selling drugs. Her mother had struggled with addiction for years. Her parents had already separated because of her excessive drug use. Once her mother was arrested, her father filed for divorce. Clara saw her mother only once when she got out of prison years later, but she lost contact as her mother sank deep into the cycle of being on the streets using then going back to jail.

While her family's makeup was different, their day-to-day life was typical. Her father had a stable middle-class job as an engineer. They were active in church, and her father was even a deacon. On the surface, they looked like so many other families, but no one knew the things he whispered to her in the dark.

She hated his words demanding silence, but she obeyed for years and years. By remaining silent, the voice of shame grew louder and louder. She always felt shame. So much so it had become her identity. The little-girl Clara held the secret tightly out of fear and love for her father. But the teenage Clara found it harder and harder to swallow the lies and shame.

The summer before their junior year in high school, Clara and her best friend, Emily, spent as much time together as possible. Sleepovers at Emily's were the highlight of any weekend they occurred. One evening after late-night-movie binge-watching and gorging on Cheetos and Reese's and beer stolen from the garage beer fridge, the two sat on the bed sharing secrets. With each new secret, the giggles would follow. After Emily shared the sordid details of her last date with her boyfriend Jacob, Clara didn't giggle. Instead, her eyes dropped to the knobby bedspread, and her fingers twisted a lone curl from her long hair.

"What is it?" Emily asked as she bounced on the bed, "Tell me, did you meet someone?"

Slightly shaking her head from side to side, Clara took a deep breath and spoke the forbidden for the first time. The bouncing stopped, and Clara looked up, expecting to see concern and support. But that was not the expression she encountered. Instead, Emily's eyebrows furrowed, and her mouth was half-open in a twisted frown as she blurted out, "Oh my gosh, that is so gross."

No denying the look of pure disgust accompanied by the question, "Your own father?"

The internal shame Clara carried was nothing compared to the shame she felt from her friend's words. Unwanted tears exploded from her eyes as she practically vaulted off the bed toward the door. Realizing her mistake, Emily ran between Clara and the door. She grabbed her friend and began repeating she was sorry and didn't mean to sound so mean. Eventually, they made it back to the bed. Clara flopped her head in Emily's lap and cried, this time with Emily gently twisting Clara's long curls. The tears weren't flowing because of the pain of what her father did. These were tears of shame. Clara regretted her disobedience. She had been warned. It was a secret. And now she understood why. The truth was evidence of her sin and would always bring judgment and shame. No matter how much comfort her friend tried to provide, the sin could not be soothed away.

Restorative Justice

Clara's search for justice began that dark night. What she didn't know then was how restorative justice would play a role in her healing. One definition for restorative justice is as follows: "Restorative Justice is a way of responding to conflict, misbehavior, and crime that makes things as right as possible for all who were impacted. Restorative Justice includes recognizing the conflict or harm, repairing the damage (physical and relational) as much as possible, and creating future accountability plans and/or agreements that will prevent the same thing from happening again. Restorative Justice includes programs, processes, and procedures that are guided by Restorative Justice Principles."[1]

Restorative justice uses trained facilitators to bring together individuals who have been harmed with the person responsible for the harm. When all the parties are adequately prepared and agree to meet, the group will work with each other to determine an appropriate outcome for all impacted, with a primary focus on repairing the harm done.

Restorative justice differs from the retributive criminal justice system in the United States. In a retributive system, four questions are asked: What laws have been broken? Who broke the law? What is the penalty for breaking that law? and Does the punishment fit the crime? Restorative justice asks three different questions: Who has been harmed? What are their needs? and Whose obligation is it to meet those needs?

In 2006 the United Nations released the *Handbook on Restorative Justice Programmes* as a part of their Criminal Justice Handbook Series. According to the handbook,

> Restorative justice programmes are based on several underlying assumptions: (a) that the response to crime should repair as much as possible the harm suffered by the victim; (b) that offenders should be brought to understand that their behaviour is not acceptable and that it had some real consequences for the victim and community; (c) that offenders can and should accept responsibility for their action; (d) that victims should have an opportunity to express their needs and to participate in determining the best way for the offender to make reparation, and (e) that the community has a responsibility to contribute to this process.[2]

There are different forms of restorative justice and a variety of processes. The two most common are

- victim-offender mediation or victim-offender dialogue and
- restorative justice circles.

Victim-offender dialogue is a one-on-one meeting between the victim and the offender, with a third party facilitating the process. In cases of severe violence, the victim initiates the victim-offender dialogue process to prevent victimization or harm. Typically, the victim-offender dialogue process is voluntary for all participants. However, preparation is also required before bringing parties together to ensure that the process will benefit all as much as possible.

Circles are another restorative justice process. Circles are a facilitated dialogue based on the assumption that people want to connect and interact with meaning. In addition to the facilitator (or circle keeper) the elements of circles include guidelines, a talking piece, and an opening and closing ceremony. The talking piece is passed around the circle counterclockwise, allowing every person to speak. Decisions are made by consensus, and the process focuses on relationships and storytelling. Circles can be a valuable tool for organizations and churches to use to begin creating opportunities for healing and understanding survivors of sexual violence. They can also be a powerful tool for addressing harm, providing accountability, and facilitating justice.

So, what makes restorative justice work? What is the process? Five crucial elements must be present in restorative justice processes:

- direct voice
- stakeholder focus
- accountability
- clarity around values
- safe/structured environment

We will look at each element in greater detail in the following chapters. As organizations and churches move forward in creating sacred space for survivors, two necessary steps must be taken:

1. Ensure all of these five elements are present in any programs or processes created.
2. Ensure all facilitators have adequate training.

The material in this book will help with developing protocols, policies, and processes. But if restorative justice processes are implemented, all facilitators of those processes need to be trained. Training is critical to ensure competency, prevent ongoing harm, and provide opportunities for repairing damage, promoting greater understanding, and bringing healing.

Element #1: Direct Voice

The first and most essential element of restorative justice is direct voice. Direct voice is when the person directly impacted by the crime, conflict, or problem has a voice in what needs to happen next. The power of direct voice is foundational to restorative justice. It allows the one harmed to ask questions for understanding and healing, to communicate the impact of the harm, and to discuss options for repairing harm when appropriate. It is also essential for the individual responsible for harming another to answer questions for understanding and healing, to understand the impact of the harm on others, and to discuss options for repairing harm when appropriate.

In a traditional court case, the victim's voice is secondary to the law. Prosecutors or investigators will interact with victims throughout the process, but their focus remains on the law. Victims are allowed to make a victim impact statement, typically at the sentencing phase of a trial. But for the most part, victims' voices are not given the attention they deserve and need. This inability to speak into the process can create a longing for true justice.

In *The Little Book of Restorative Justice*, Howard Zehr talks about four needs that seem to be neglected in our traditional court system. They are information, truth-telling, empowerment, and restitution.[3] The first two needs addressed by Zehr can be met when all the individuals impacted by the harm are given a voice. People need information and want answers to questions. Why did this happen? What details were involved? Do you know what you did? In the typical court process, these answers are rarely found.

We can provide opportunities for the Claras of the world to share their stories and seek truth and healing. As we learn more about restorative justice and evaluate our role in creating a sacred space for survivors of sexual assault like Clara, we can bring the light of healing. We can create opportunities for survivors of sexual assault to rightly place the shame on the one who caused the harm and the one who must own up to the reality of the harm they have done. Truth-telling is significant for survivors. Those who cause the harm rarely understand or truly grasp the extent of that harm. Clara is a beautiful example of the yearning to be heard. There was a hunger, a passion for sharing about the devastation and suffering she endured. But, her sharing wasn't just about the desire to speak and the desperation for truth. As we will learn in later chapters, in telling her story, Clara holds her father responsible for the crime of ravaging a five-year-old child over and over. In telling her story, truth is revealed.

Element #2: Stakeholder Focus

As we read in Clara's story, her father's actions played a significant role in her ongoing trauma. But what must not be missed is that Clara was not the only person impacted by the trauma. As we will learn in coming chapters, that shame and pain continued into her adult life, affecting her children and husband. Having survived being abused as a child, the last thing Clara wanted to do was become an abuser herself. She did not abuse her children physically, but they were still forced to share in her trauma.

When a crime is committed, we can quickly identify the primary victim or victims directly impacted by the crime. But there are also secondary and tertiary victims that are affected. Most victim-offender dialogue processes target the direct victim as well as secondary victims. An example of this might be the survivor of a sexual assault—the initial victim—and the partner or child of that survivor—the secondary victims.

Stakeholders are all the individuals impacted by an event. Identifying and understanding stakeholders creates more significant opportunities for holistic healing. A comprehensive approach could include creating space for personal healing through therapeutic one-on-one counseling sessions and opportunities for secondary victims. This can also include opportunities for partners and children to access services like counseling or restorative justice processes. Including the one who committed harm brings the stakeholder concept full circle.

An often-neglected stakeholder is the family of the one committing the crime or harm. If the offender is sentenced to prison, their family shares that sentence. Countless mothers and fathers are ashamed and saddened by the actions of their children. Numerous children will be raised without a parent. Families are forced to develop relationships through letters and prison visits. Some never asked for the reality they must live.

A participant in a victim-offender dialogue shared her reason for wanting to participate in the process. She explained she had her story as the victim of how the crime impacted her life and the devastation she suffered. Likewise, she said her offender has a story about how the crime impacted his life since he is now in prison. But she wanted the opportunity to write the final chapter of their story of what it means to them together. Her motivation is a beautiful example of the importance of having all the voices and stakeholders in the dialogue and healing process.

Justice for the Suffering

What Clara experienced at the hands of her father was horrific. When we hear stories like hers, we may ask, where was the justice? Why didn't anyone intervene? Did she ever find justice? In the following chapters, we will continue with Clara's story to learn the answers to those questions. An important question to ask first is, What is justice? While we can categorize the many forms of justice like social justice or criminal justice, it is more important to ask where the journey for justice begins. Every pursuit of justice starts somewhere—a sacred text, a social rule, or personal pain. Often these starting points overlap.

- Pursuing an understanding of justice through sacred texts (sacral)
- Pursuing a form of justice defined by societal rules and laws (societal/judicial)
- Pursuing a sense of justice based on need and pain (personal)

This concept of three is not found in most explanations of restorative justice. But it is important to note because in reality, it is at the root of why those who have experienced violence and trauma are motivated to do more than just seek justice through typical means. The reality is that the pursuit for justice will be linked to one of these three starting points and is addressed differently in each. But there can be an overlap between them, as shown in the diagram below.

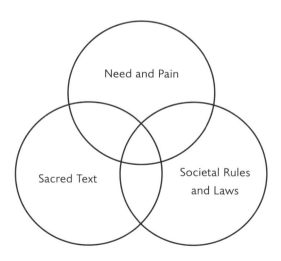

We see the overlap between the Ten Commandments in the sacred text of Exodus and the laws in our modern criminal and civil justice systems or societal laws. "Thou shalt not kill" (Exod. 20:13 KJV) translates to the prosecution of murder in our criminal justice system. "Thou shalt not bear false witness against thy neighbor" (Exod. 20:16 KJV) can be seen as slander in our civil and criminal justice systems. While there may be overlap, each source of justice is different and accomplishes different outcomes.

But there is that sweet spot in the middle where all three pursuits of justice are fulfilled. This perfect spot happens when the court system works and the one who did the harm is held accountable according to society's laws; then, when that system overlaps with a survivor working through the spiritual aspects from a supportive church and understanding the complexities of faith around harm and forgiveness; and finally, when the survivor has the opportunity to define justice based on personal needs and the pain caused. When survivors have a direct voice, all stakeholders are involved in a safer place where accountability is practiced, and values are honored, true justice is found.

Sacral Justice

Some survivors pursue justice based on sacred truth like the Bible. God addresses justice from Genesis to Revelation. The prophets called for justice; psalmists penned God's heart for the hurting and oppressed and the call to do what is just and right. It is first seen in Genesis after God creates Adam and Eve. Their first offspring, the first to be *born* of man, are Cain and Abel. It is the firstborn of man who introduces the concepts of justice and injustice into the world through the act of murder. Interestingly, the first story attributed to the firstborn of man is a story of crime and justice. This story is not about just any crime; it is a crime of greatest devastation—murder.

Genesis 4:8–12 tells the story of Abel's murder and what justice demanded.

> Now Cain said to his brother Abel, "Let's go out to the field." While they were in the field, Cain attacked his brother Abel and killed him.
>
> Then the LORD said to Cain, "Where is your brother Abel?"
>
> "I don't know," he replied. "Am I my brother's keeper?"
>
> The LORD said, "What have you done? Listen! Your brother's blood cries out to me from the ground. Now you are under a curse and driven from the ground, which opened its mouth to receive your brother's blood from your hand. When you work the ground, it will no longer yield its crops for you. You will be a restless wanderer on the earth."

God saw the crime and called Cain to account, asking, "What have you done?" Cain does not acknowledge his guilt, but God does. God demands justice on behalf of Abel in two ways. The first is he pronounces the verdict in the form of a curse. But God further demands that Cain listen to Abel's cries, cries for justice. Abel's blood cried out to God, demanding justice.

Christ's arrival into the world, when he dwelt among us, echoes the message of the importance of justice to God. Matthew 12:17–21 says:

> This was to fulfill what was spoken through the prophet Isaiah:
>
> > "Here is my servant whom I have chosen,
> >   the one I love, in whom I delight;
> > I will put my Spirit on him,
> >   and he will proclaim justice to the nations.
> > He will not quarrel or cry out;
> >   no one will hear his voice in the streets.

A bruised reed he will not break,
 and a smoldering wick he will not snuff out,
till he has brought justice through to victory.
 In his name, the nations will put their hope."

Matthew writes that Jesus will proclaim justice. A proclamation is something spoken. We can take action to enforce justice, just like God did when he cursed Cain and made him a restless wanderer. It is words that facilitate justice in both passages. There is no escaping the call for justice found in the sacred truth of the Bible. What does that look like today, particularly in the church? It is a hope that this book will provide some resources that will equip leaders and churches to explore greater ways to facilitate justice with a focus on survivors of sexual violence.

Societal/Judicial Justice

Many survivors pursue justice based on society's laws. There are volumes of books on laws and processes. But unlike biblical truth, laws written by men can be challenged and rewritten. Laws were created to protect and allow "liberty and justice for all." As society changes, the laws that govern the people also change. New laws emerge out of a need to address new issues. For example, laws about cybercrime were unheard of fifty years ago.

We operate with a retributive justice model for our criminal justice system in the United States. This comes from the idea that punishment, when proportionally appropriate, is an acceptable response to crime and injustice. A person found guilty of a crime in our existing justice system is not expected to take responsibility for their actions. A person can be sentenced to life in prison for a particular crime due to the evidence and never admit guilt. An admission of guilt is not a requirement for the pronouncement of guilt. Because the retributive justice system does not hold the one who committed the crime to a standard of personal accountability for his or her actions, that place of ambiguity between convicted guilt and admitted guilt becomes a chasm where victims can get caught.

Personal Justice

When justice is pursued based on pain or needs, it becomes much more complex. Victims of crime or injustice may seek justice through our civil and criminal justice system. But there may be times when survivors choose not to work through the court systems. One woman who was sexually abused by her father explained she never wanted her father to go to jail. She only wanted him to stop what he was doing to her. Victims may also seek insight into justice from sacred texts like the Bible. But they may still feel justice has not been met, thoroughly answered, or wholly fulfilled by either the courts or the Bible. It is not heresy to say that someone cannot find the answer to a need in the Bible alone.

Many states have a victim-offender dialogue program where victims of violent crimes can meet face-to-face with the offender who committed the crime. In each case, the person convicted of the crime is serving or has served their sentence. So, according to the laws of society, justice has been done—the person responsible was convicted and punished. But over and over, victims still seek more. Thousands of individuals have reached out to meet with their offenders face-to-face. They seek more justice than what is accomplished through society's laws.

Some in the victim-offender dialogue process are members of faith institutions and have processed the crime through sacred texts and wrestled with their faith to realize justice has still not been served. Yet, many victims search for more, for that day of reckoning, where accounts are put right. There may be an unmet need such as a need to find answers that only the offender can provide, a need to articulate to the offender exactly how the crime has impacted their life, or a need to have their pain acknowledged. Some victims need their offenders to know the depth of pain caused by the crime, not only to the primary victim but also the pain to the secondary and tertiary victims. These needs cannot be met through the courts or the church. They can be met only through a direct voice like that provided in the victim-offender dialogue process or circles, by facing the one who created the pain. And overwhelmingly, victims who meet with the one who committed the harm find significant healing and peace after participating in these face-to-face meetings.

As Christians, we are not doing an adequate job assisting survivors of sexual violence. But it does not have to stay that way. Sadly, many victims seeking to participate in restorative justice programs like victim-offender dialogue have heard some version of a statement such as, "You just need to forgive them like the Bible says, then move on." But forgiveness is not an act of justice; it is an act of mercy. Forgiveness can be a part of the healing journey, but justice demands more. That is why it becomes crucial to create opportunities to explore healing through all means of justice—sacral, societal/judicial, and personal. The church should take the command of Christ seriously to be ministers of reconciliation and provide processes and opportunities that can facilitate healing and justice.

The Bible does not provide details about the murder of Abel, but it does provide the consequences. His murder was a crime that demanded justice, demanded attention, demanded action. So God pronounced that Cain was cursed as a result of his crime. But don't miss the fact that God also demanded that Cain listen to the voice of his victim—his brother—crying out. A passage about justice emerging from pain or need is tucked away in this very first story. It vividly details the need to listen to the cries, the pain, of Abel.

The emotions, pain, or trauma a person feels from the crime or injustice committed against them is not easily measured. For example, how do we determine the punishment for a five-year-old girl's sorrow after being repeatedly violated by her father? Society's laws would be hard-pressed to attempt to measure and articulate that sorrow. But we must begin seeking and creating processes that address all the effects of crime and injustice on individuals. Restorative justice is the most logical starting place.

CHAPTER 2

Owning Your Stuff

Creepy was Clara's first thought as the three men walked into the room to sit at the large plastic white table. All three were part of an offender panel about to speak at the Victim Offender Symposium. The symposium was hosted by the victim services department in her state. It was held annually for victims and those who work with them to gather and learn. Clara had spoken on a victim impact panel earlier in the symposium, and her nerves were fried. She thought back to the shame she felt the night she first told her story to her best friend. But she no longer felt shame. It was just the opposite; now she found healing in sharing her story.

She first found that healing at a support group at her church for survivors of sexual violence. Her little community church was the first place she felt safe. That was not something she felt in other churches in the past; in fact it was rare. She learned more about God and his love for her in the two years she attended this church than she had any other time in her life despite being a frequent churchgoer.

The leader of the church support group had asked participants if any were interested in speaking on a panel about surviving sexual violence and the impact of the crime. Clara's first reaction to thinking about speaking in public about such a shameful experience was panic. She imagined telling her story and looking into the audience and seeing the same disgust she saw in her friend's face the first time she broke the silence rule. But the leader explained that telling their stories can be healing and even empowering. Several others who had agreed to participate confirmed how powerful the process was. Clara was intrigued. Finally she mustered the courage to do it.

Today was the third time she participated in a panel. And it was true: every time she told her story, she was reminded how strong she was and how she survived. It was empowering, but it was also emotionally draining.

When the three men walked into the room Clara wanted to rush back to her hotel room and sit alone in the dark to calm down. But instead, her friend insisted that she sit in on the offender-panel workshop this afternoon.

The room for this session was tiny. Clara sat in the very last row with her back against the wall. She scanned the room and noticed that it was beginning to fill. If she wanted to leave and skip this session for the coolness of her hotel, it would have to be soon. They were adding more chairs to accommodate the people crowding in. If she waited too much longer, she would not be able to get through the crowd to get out. Before she made up her mind, her friend walked in and sat next to her. The moderator began and introduced the three men. She was stuck.

The moderator explained the process. The panelists would share their crimes and what they had done since release. The first to speak was Robert, a man convicted of sexual assault. He served fifteen years before being released. He didn't know the victim. He saw her at a bar and thought she was so beautiful. He watched her all night but never mustered the courage to speak to her. Instead, when she left, he followed her home. He sat outside her house for several hours, trying to convince himself to leave. But his desire to see her asleep was too overwhelming. Finally, he found an unlocked window and slipped inside.

He said, "The next thing I knew, I was on top of her, raping her."

She fought him and, in the process, dug her fingernails into his flesh. The DNA from the rape kit was enough to convict him, and he was sentenced to twenty years in prison. During that time, he attended sex-offender treatment, grappled with his horrible crime, and made follow-up plans to ensure he never re-offended.

The second person recounted a similar crime.

The last one to speak was a short, chubby man named Thomas. His salt-and-pepper hair had receded several inches, making his forehead look huge. It didn't help that he wore black-rimmed glasses that reminded her of her nerdy ninth-grade algebra teacher. His wrinkled plaid shirt had seen a few too many washings. Something about him was very unsettling for Clara. Finally, the moderator asked Thomas to talk about his crime. "I sexually assaulted my six-year-old daughter." He hesitated before adding, "for more than four years." Clara stopped breathing. Her eyes locked on Thomas. The soft touch from her friend on her arm made Clara gasp, and she realized she had not been breathing. Thomas continued to describe his crime. When his daughters were very young, his wife was killed in a car accident. About a year after his wife's death, Thomas began to watch his daughter Lily. He knew the way he looked at her was wrong. And that was when the lies in his head began. *She looked at him the same way he looked at her. She wanted him to be closer. She needed him to love her more.* Finally, after several months of trying to resist the lies, he gave in.

He recounted how he finally entered her small bedroom that first night more than twenty years ago.

Clara spiraled into a screaming panic. She looked around the room, worried she had caused a scene. But no one was moving; the screams were only in her head. Thomas went on to say how he knew when he walked through his daughter's door that night that what he was about to do was evil and horribly wrong. He cried and explained he knew it was sick and how much he had destroyed his daughter's life. He wept as he recounted her haunted eyes those nights in her room, knowing he was the monster in her life. That was it; Clara was undone. Her eyes darted from Thomas to the door. *Why did they put the table between the audience and the door?* she wondered. There was no escape. She was trapped. The pounding and throbbing of her pulse in her ears had to be audible to others. She couldn't calm her breathing. Alarms sounded in her mind as she tried not to spiral further into hysteria. She jerked toward her friend, hoping she could see the panic and do something. But her wide eyes made it clear she was just as helpless to do anything. Her eyes went back to Thomas as he ended the session by saying, "I am so ashamed of what I did." When Clara heard those words, two possibilities flashed simultaneously in her mind. One was to rush up to the table, dig her fingers into Thomas's face, and gouge out his eyes. The other was to rush to the table, hug him, and kiss his cheek. Wanting both of those things at the same time was almost unbearable. But both were true. She hated him for what he did, for what he represented. And she was freaked out by the strange, unwanted love that made her want to kiss his cheek. He acknowledged his guilt and told the truth that he was a monster. Clara would have given anything for her own father to do what Thomas just did and tell the truth.

With that realization, she closed her eyes and willed herself to calm down as much as possible until this nightmare was over. Fifteen minutes later, she was sitting with her friend in a small alcove in the back of the hotel lobby. After a few minutes, they decided it would be best if Clara found one of the volunteer counselors at the symposium, and off they went. After meeting with the counselor, Clara agreed to reach out to her therapist.

Several weeks later, during a counseling session, her therapist suggested the idea of Clara mediating with Thomas. She explained there was a program called Making It Right in which men convicted of sexual assault volunteered as surrogates to do mediations with victims of similar crimes. Most of the victims who participated in Making It Right did so because their offenders were never prosecuted or were dead or the crime was never reported. Not being able to talk to (or meet with) the person who harmed caused many to have questions left unanswered. Some victims didn't have questions; they just wanted the opportunity to tell someone how much they screwed up their life. The therapist had referred other patients to Making It Right, and she knew Thomas participated.

Clara's father died during her junior year. He was diagnosed with cancer in the fall of that year and was gone within six months. When Clara's father passed away they hadn't spoken in over a year. The finality of never hearing him admit what he had done was a burden Clara desperately wanted to shed. When the therapist suggested a surrogate mediation, Clara wanted to say no, but she felt that same mixed feeling the day she heard Thomas speak. But this time, that love/hate mash-up was also mixed with terror and hope at the prospect of meeting with Thomas. She knew she had to do it.

Element #3: Accountability

One of the significant components of the restorative justice processes and victim-offender dialogues, like Making It Right, is the need for accountability. In victim-offender dialogue, personal responsibility and accountability by the one who committed the crime are prerequisites for participation. If that person does not take responsibility, the process is stopped because face-to-face meetings can potentially create further harm. This concept of accountability is not just found in victim-offender dialogue processes; it is also found in Scripture.

According to 1 John 1:9, there is a necessity for confession and acknowledgment of sin that sets into motion the process of reconciliation with a righteous and just God: "If we confess our sins, He is faithful and just to forgive us our sins and to cleanse us from all unrighteousness" (NKJV). If accountability to the point of confession is necessary for reconciliation with God, we should also see the necessity for accountability in human interactions. Not taking responsibility keeps the truth in the shadows. Thomas was willing to escape the darkness of his lies and vile acts. Thomas's willingness to take full responsibility for the damage he did to his daughter set Clara on a path toward mediation.

We all want people to own up to what they did when they hurt us. How to accomplish this can be a challenge. First, we must develop skills to help people see their responsibility for harm. But before we can help others these skills need to be practiced and applied on a personal level. It is easy to see when *other* people don't take responsibility for the harm they have done. But we need to be intentional about owning our wrong acts, too. As facilitators, as family members, as friends, as coworkers, taking responsibility and acknowledging our own wrongs should be a lifestyle choice. It is difficult to admit when we are wrong. All you have to do is to think back on a time when you knew you hurt someone else and knew it needed to be made right. Most likely, it did not feel good to acknowledge your actions and take steps to repair the harm. But, while it may be momentarily uncomfortable, pushing past discomfort, admitting guilt, and taking responsibility will allow for more significant opportunities for growth and integrity.

As a facilitator, addressing accountability must begin in one of two places. It begins either within a relationship or with another person's willingness to engage in a dialogue about their crime or harm. In victim-offender dialogue, offenders voluntarily agree to participate, knowing that responsibility is a part of the process. Because of the offender's willingness to participate, the mediator is invited to speak and challenge the offender. The same is true in other relationships. Attempting to force personal accountability outside of relationships can create feelings of judgment from those who have not requested that input. Therefore, the first step in helping someone own their harm is cultivating a relationship where that person would eventually be open to more candid conversations.

Lack of Accountability

When there is ongoing conflict or tension, the reason may be that someone in the situation is not accepting responsibility for the harm done. When this occurs, the natural human instinct is to build an emotional wall to protect us from future damage. While that is not how we are intended to interact with one another, it is a human instinct and method of survival. So, when we get hurt, we naturally try to protect ourselves from future hurt.

We easily recognize this whenever we experience physical pain. You put your bare hand on a hot skillet handle and burn yourself; the next time, you protect yourself using a potholder. We instinctively do the same with emotional hurts. Unfortunately, if we are hurt too often without opportunities for healing and reparations, the result may be cynicism or bitterness.

Moving toward accountability risks pain because we make ourselves vulnerable to the other person. Pain is one of the reasons people shy away from conflict and prefer either to avoid the conflict or to force an issue. As we work with others to find the truth, we sometimes need to encourage people to lean into the pain as a path to healing or understanding others who view the world differently.

The fastest way to address accountability begins in its absence. People who have knowingly hurt others and refuse to take responsibility for their actions are dangerous. If they don't see anything wrong with their harmful behavior, there is little reason to change it. This is why a lack of accountability has the potential to be dangerous.

Nobody likes to admit they are wrong. Unfortunately, human nature causes us to try and avoid shame or harm by making excuses, blaming others, or justifying and minimizing our actions. The good news is that we can develop the ability to hear these thinking errors in ourselves and in others who have caused harm. While we use hundreds of thinking errors to keep from taking responsibility, we will highlight only the most common.

Common Thinking Errors

Making excuses. Thinking there is a reason for everything and anything. You carefully concentrate on the reason or the excuse why something has happened rather than accepting responsibility for it. For example, "My family was rich." Or "My family was poor." Or "I've never been able to read very well."

Blaming. Blaming others for your actions and portraying yourself as a victim. When you blame others, you are no longer responsible. "I did take it, but he told me to." Or "I knew it was a lie, but she told me to tell you that."

Minimizing. Making something big into something small. Minimizing is a common denial technique used to convince yourself to believe that what you've done is not really important or bad. "At least I didn't molest children in my own family." "I took only twenty dollars; they have plenty of money."

Justifying. Explaining the reason for things. For example, "He wasn't my natural son, just my stepson." Or "My wife wouldn't have sex with me. So what's a man to do?"

Re-defining or hopping over. Shifting the focus of an issue to avoid solving the problem. Re-defining allows you to avoid examining the real issue. For example, "Why didn't you do your assignment this week?" Answer: "I've done my assignment for the last three weeks."

Seeking sympathy. Thinking others should sympathize and feel sorry for you. You will feel better if you can get others to feel sorry for you. For example, "Why should I ask questions? My questions are never right." Or "My family would be better off without me."

Assuming. Believing that you are so powerful that you know how others think and feel. Typically, assumers do not check the facts or care what other people think and feel. Arrogantly, you assume what others are thinking. "I didn't call because I knew she thought I was a bad person."

Victimizing. Presenting yourself as a victim. It is a way to manipulate others using passive-aggressive behavior, often with people who care about you. For example, "I may have been driving drunk, but I was the only one who got hurt in the accident."

Lying. Telling untruths to confuse, distort, and make fools of other people. Lying is one of the most common thinking errors and is done in many different ways. There are three kinds of lies: making up things that are not true; stating partly true things, but leaving out certain details; and behaving or acting in a way that isn't accurate or suggests something that isn't true (for instance, you show support for someone else when, in fact, you are actually critical of that person).

Once we are aware of all these thinking errors, it is easy to see when we use them ourselves. The telltale sign that a thinking error is about to appear is the word "but" in an apology. "I know I did it, but . . ." Knowing what to look for when helping others take personal responsibility takes time and practice. Begin by listening to others as they discuss their role in a conflict.

Disclaimers

There are several disclaimers about accountability. First, just because a person does not take responsibility does not mean some form of justice can't be pursued. And it may be necessary to take steps as a society to hold that person responsible for their actions even if they won't do so themselves. This is where the legal system should be utilized.

Another disclaimer is that sometimes the lack of an admission of guilt, or personal accountability, does NOT prevent reconciliation or continued relationships. This happens between friends or spouses all the time. For example, there may be a conflict where each person feels the other is wrong, but neither will admit their perspective or actions are incorrect. Instead, they decide the relationship is too important to allow those differences to be an ongoing issue, and they are put aside. In this case, it helps to acknowledge our differences in a way that each person agrees that the relationship is more important.

Truth-telling

Sexual violence creates wounds that may not be visible. In some cases, survivors suffer physical injuries like beatings, stabbings, burns, or gunshots, all of which leave physical scars. But for many, the wounds of sexual violence are not physical and are invisible to others.

In 2004, three women participated in a victim impact panel. The Victim Support Program invited them to share their stories with a group of parolees and staff of the parole office in their community. One victim detailed a violent rape where she was stabbed multiple times and beaten about the head with a rock. In her story, she shared the months it took to recover, and the physical and emotional scars of that attack are always with her.

Another woman on the panel shared a story similar to Clara's, where a family member sexually abused her for several years before she finally told someone. The man was subsequently arrested and convicted. His conviction split up their family. Even though the man pleaded guilty due to the overwhelming evidence indicating that he had committed the crime, he told his family members the charges were false, and the woman was lying. He convinced them she was the liar, and she made it all up. He said he took the plea bargain only out of fear of possible conviction with a massive sentence. She went on to share that, to this day, she still has no contact with close family members who support the man in prison. After sharing her story, she looked at the woman who spoke first and said, "I wish I had a physical scar. If I had a scar, no one could deny the vicious act that happened to me. If I had a scar, they would know the truth. I am not the liar."

Truth-telling is powerful. Thomas was being truthful about his crime and the impact he had on his daughter's life. Clara was not the person Thomas harmed, but the simple fact that she heard him take responsibility and speak the truth set her on a life-altering journey, as seen in the following chapters. Thomas came to the place of owning his truth, as ugly as it was, because he willingly agreed to participate in the restorative justice process of Making It Right. Thomas first learned of the program in prison when his cellmate participated in a meeting with the person against whom he committed his crime. Thomas wanted the opportunity to meet with his daughter and wrote to the program. He was told that Making It Right is a victim-centered program that can be initiated only by a victim. But his letter would be added to a bank of other letters from perpetrators. They also explained that he had an option of participating in surrogate mediations if he chose, for which he readily volunteered. Two years later he met with his daughter, at her request. Since then, he also partic- ipated in one previous surrogate mediation before meeting with Clara. We may never know if he would have arrived at the place of full accountability without the program. But we know for sure the program required that he must.

This is why it is essential to understand the power of account- ability and learn the skills to help others discover it. Redirecting or correcting thinking errors is a way to help people move toward greater accountability. The principles used in situations of crime can be used practically in everyday situations involving conflict and harm. When someone makes a statement like, "It was an ac- cident," you can ask the question, "What do you think the person you harmed would think hearing you call what happened an 'ac- cident'?" If someone makes a minimizing statement like, "I took only twenty dollars; they have plenty of money," you can ask, "Are you saying it is okay to steal money as long as it is from someone who has more money than you?" Asking simple questions like these can help people realize their thinking errors.

We can also role-play scenarios based on what might happen when they meet with the person they harmed. For instance, if someone wants to make things right, you may ask, "What will you do if you apologize and your friend is still angry?" The answer to a role-play like that will demonstrate the level of accountability the one harming is taking. If they respond with a comment like, "I will just listen," or "I will take it because I caused that anger," you know there is accountability. If they respond with a comment like, "It will make me mad," the conversation should shift to help that individual understand their connection and responsibility for the victim's anger.

Try it out. There are so many opportunities in our day-to-day lives where we hear people make excuses for their harmful be- havior. Begin to listen for those thinking errors and use moments in everyday conversations to practice helping people hear their words. And remember, a telltale word for thinking errors is "but." "I know I hurt her, but . . ."

You can begin by practicing with your own words. Then, start becoming aware of when you do it. For example, when you use phrases to apologize like "but I was only trying to . . ." or "it's just that . . ." or "I did that only because . . ." you may be minimizing or making excuses. But, fortunately, the more we practice it, the more we will hear how our erroneous thinking comes sneaking out in words used to ease the discomfort of our actions.

There is power in truth and in acknowledging the harm we have done. And it takes work to communicate that responsibility in the fullness of truth without all the thinking errors we typically display. But, when someone says, "I know I hurt you. I am so very sorry. Can I do anything to make things right?" it is almost like the earth itself breathes a heavy sigh.

CHAPTER 3

Understanding the Ripples of Denial

It doesn't burn. It doesn't burn, Clara repeated to herself as she stood beside the antique white stove in her off-campus apartment near the University of Texas at Dallas (UTD). Looking at the skillet of hot grease on the burner, Clara clenched her teeth as she dipped a spoon to scoop up the scalding oil and poured it on the inside of her forearm. *It doesn't burn. It doesn't burn.* She didn't know why it made her feel better when something hurt so bad, but bizarrely, it did. After a few more spoonfuls she grabbed her keys and headed to the Student Health Services Clinic. But, of course, she lied to the nurse and said she spilled a pan of grease on her arm. They tended to her second-degree burn, wrapped it up, and sent her home. By the time she woke up the following day, the blister under the gauze was the size of an avocado bulging off her arm.

Clara distinctly remembered the first time she had intentionally mutilated herself. She was in the third grade and fell off her bike on the driveway. As she slipped, her cheek hit the side of the garage door. Tears streaming down her face, she ran inside to her father. He sat in his gray recliner, feet propped up and ankles crossed as he watched a football game. Clara ran to him and threw herself over his arm, plopping the right side of her face in his lap so he could see the horrible wound on her cheek. He was displeased by the interruption and, with little effort, lifted her off and pushed her back. Then, with a glance, he told her to go back outside. She was fine.

"There's only a small red spot. You will be fine." Why didn't he pick her up like other dads and hold her until she felt better? Why didn't he love her? He said he loved her whenever he came to her room at night. He said they had the most special love, but she didn't understand. He didn't even take the time to look closer to make sure she was okay. Finally, she decided she would show him.

Clara went outside and found a smooth brown speckled rock that perfectly fit her hand. She went to the tool closet in the back of the garage and tucked herself into the far corner where shadows hid her tiny frame. With her eight-year-old determination, she took the rock and smacked herself on the cheek. She expected it to hurt like it did when she fell off the bike, but it wasn't that bad. It hurt, but it also made her feel powerful. That power fueled her to hit herself over and over and over. *He is going to feel bad when he sees this.*

Afterward, she played alone with her Barbies on the garage floor until her father told her to come inside for dinner. She was ever so pleased with herself when he looked at her and started to look away before snapping his head back to see her face. He quickly rushed to her, dropped to his knee, and said, "Oh baby, you did do a number on yourself. Let's get that cleaned up." And for the next few minutes, he wiped her face, got an ice pack to help with the swelling, and even offered to take her to McDonald's for a Happy Meal.

That day Clara found a surefire way to get her father's attention and love. He teased her about being such a klutz and always getting banged up. Little did he know how nonklutzy and meticulously planned her injuries were. The destructive behaviors continued into her adolescence and adulthood. Hurting herself took on many forms. As a teenager, she added alcohol, weed, and promiscuous behavior to her arsenal. It was easy to get away with drinking and partying because, by her teenage years, her father paid little attention to her. He hardly looked at her, but boy, he looked at her friends. She rarely invited her friends to her house because she couldn't stand to see her father's glazed-over eyes and his slimy half smile as he stared without shame at her friend's breasts.

Almost every weekend, she would find somewhere to spend the night. And if she picked the right friend, they could sneak out, get drunk or high or both and hang out with guys all night. Her dad would encourage her to have her friends stay at their house, but there was no way she would give him the satisfaction.

Despite all the partying and unhealthy behavior, Clara graduated from high school. She was shocked when she got her acceptance letter from UTD since her grades were so-so. But she was thrilled because it was well-known as a party school. Not to mention, she would be free of her father.

The freedom of college created a perfect backdrop for Clara's life to spin out of control. The first semester was good. She balanced the partying and drugs with completing her coursework. She had to drop a class in the second semester to keep from failing. But it wasn't just the partying that made it difficult for Clara to focus on school. There were days she could not get out of bed because of her heaviness and sorrow. Depressed, she lay in bed in the dark dreaming of ways to end her life.

On one of those dark nights she told her roommate, "If you could cut my chest open and look inside, you would see nothing but six inches of black soot."

In her mind's eye, Clara saw layers of blackness coating her ribcage and entire inner torso. But like the self-mutilation, somehow, the sadness was comforting, like a comfortable blanket. Like the kind you have had for years and feels soft not only from the worn familiarity but also soft from the memories of holding little girl tears.

By the middle of her sophomore year Clara was spinning out of control. She ricocheted from thinking obsessively of ending her life to partying excessively, to sleeping around with anybody who would stay with her, and to skipping classes. The first of her three suicide attempts happened that semester. She intentionally drank an excessive amount of alcohol while ingesting a handful of diazepam. Her roommates found her and called the ambulance. Clara woke up several hours later in the emergency room and was released later that day when she promised to seek counseling. Somewhere inside, she knew she needed help or she might not make it. Finally, after wrestling with whether she wanted help or was ready to end her own life, she decided to give help a try. The next day she made an appointment with Student Services Counseling. Her counselor was the most tender person Clara had ever met, and she liked her instantly. They met weekly, and Clara started to make progress. The counselor also asked if she had ever confronted her father about what he did. She had not and was terrified by the thought of it, but also instinctively knew she must.

After several weeks of preparation, the day finally came to confront her father. She invited him over saying she wanted to talk to him about something. When he questioned what it was, she just said she was thinking about her life and wanted his insight. She was afraid to give him too much information or he wouldn't even bother to make the short forty-five-minute drive to her apartment.

When he arrived they talked for a few minutes before she suggested they go out back to enjoy the beautiful spring day. They sat on the blue plastic Adirondack chairs on her tiny porch in the back of her apartment. Clara knew today was the day, and without hesitation, she began. For five minutes, Clara spewed all her rage, hatred, and anger for what he had done to her, demanding he admit to all he had done.

She screamed at him, "I remember every single night you came into my room. And if I ever mentioned anything about it, you acted like nothing happened, pretending I was the crazy one. So why would you deny something in the morning that we both knew good and well you did the night before?"

Staring at her father, she expected him to be angry like he always was when she was little. What she did not expect were her father's cocked head and puzzled expression. Instead, his half-open mouth, feigning shock, stopped her in her tracks.

Placing his hand on his chest and acting shocked, he said, "What are you talking about? I could never do something like that." His words should have pushed her into a further rage, but instead, she felt like a little five-year-old girl seeing her monster for the umpteenth time. She sat there numb as he went on and on, asking who put such thoughts in her head and how she could even think he could do something like that. Finally, he got up to leave, saying he would not sit there and listen to any more lies.

As he walked back through the apartment, going on and on about his disappointment with her accusations, he opened the door to leave. With his hand on the knob, he turned and ended with a statement that stuck with Clara forever, "Besides, why would someone admit to something that could get them sent to prison." With that, he was gone.

The encounter was not what Clara expected. She had hoped he would acknowledge how much harm he had done to her. She hoped he would realize how deeply hurt and messed up she was because of him. But instead, he did what he always did, turned things around back on her; she was the crazy one. How could she be so naive? She really thought he would do the right thing. But she also knew he never did any right thing. How could she be so stupid?

She stopped talking to her father for several months after that. But at the beginning of her junior year, he was diagnosed with cancer and died six months later. The grief process was strange for her. She was surprised she was sad he was gone. But even more surprising was her anger that she would never hear him admit guilt or ask for forgiveness. Those first few years of college were filled with so much craziness that it was a miracle she even held it together as well as she did.

Continuing school after her father's death was hard, but Clara graduated and found a job with a local bank. It didn't pay well, so she worked weekends at a local restaurant. It was there she met her husband, Tony. Once they started dating, they were inseparable, and within a year, they were married. Clara's new family looked nothing like her family growing up. They seemed pretty normal. Within four years they had three children. While their family felt normal, Clara still experienced episodes of rage, depression, and self-mutilation. Some days her rage spewed out on Tony, other days on her children over the smallest mistake.

Even though she loved her husband, Clara never felt she could fully drop her guard. He said he loved her but so did her father and he turned on her. All through her marriage she felt as if she were just holding her breath waiting for the day when he would turn on her and hurt her like her father. She thought her father truly loved her until the night he came into her room. Tony said he loved her, and she felt his love, but what if he changed one night? She knew she was cheating Tony by never loving him fully, but she couldn't. The risk of him hurting her like her father had was the dark hand that stuffed true love into a locked cubby in her heart.

Tony knew about the childhood abuse, but not in great detail. And he was completely clueless about how to help. In reality, she didn't want his help. She was afraid if he knew all her rage and hatred he would know how crazy she was and leave her. She thought back to that day on her back porch; it was more than just a day of anger and rage. She hated her father that day. It was a day of disgusting denial. Clara wasn't sure which was worse, the dark nights she endured his attacks or his obnoxious denial in the sunlit afternoon on her porch.

Element #4: Clarity around Values

Values are the beliefs that motivate people, they are the elements that act as a guide to how we will live our lives. Values can be expressed as ideas or feelings about the worth of things. When an individual values something, they think that it is worth having, worth defending, worth seeking, or worth doing. Everyone has values whether they are aware of them or not. Values, whether conscious or unconscious, are a standard by which people tend to judge the behavior, thoughts, and ideas of others. As facilitators, we can look for clues to a person's values in ideas expressed verbally and in feelings expressed either verbally or behaviorally. Examples of some common values are

- compassion,
- courage,
- determination,
- empathy,
- generosity,
- honesty,
- integrity,
- kindness,
- loyalty,
- tolerance,
- toughness, and
- trustworthiness.

Positions vs. Interest

A very critical skill in the restorative justice process is understanding the difference between positions and interests. *Positions* are the demands, the "bottom lines" that disputants present in a conflict.

Positions are typically nonnegotiable. *Interests* are the values, concerns, and needs motivating each person. When people in conflict take differing positions on an issue, disputants frequently reach an impasse, which makes negotiation and resolution impossible. One of the critical skills of a facilitator is helping people recognize the underlying needs and interests, which usually includes the values that lead them to take the positions they do on a particular issue. This can be one of the most time-consuming facets of facilitation since there is such a huge variety of needs and values. A facilitator may identify a particular need of an individual, but that doesn't necessarily mean that is the underlying need in the particular conflict. For example, a person who has been harmed by another may have an underlying unmet interest (need) for safety. But that individual could also have a variety of other interests (values or concerns) like integrity and honesty. The difference is that the *interests* of integrity and honesty are not the values or concerns motivating the person to take the position that they take. In conflict situations, if the facilitator identifies a need but the person continues to maintain the original position, the interest has not been met. The only way to identify the underlying interest is to continue to ask questions, seeking clarity until the solution can be met based on that *interest* so that the *position* is no longer first and foremost.

A goal of restorative justice is not only to identify the interests of individuals impacted by a particular situation but also to provide space for people to create solutions based on fulfilling those interests (needs and values). Any solutions or agreements that need to be made must begin with addressing interests and needs. Once this is done, the positions then become negotiable. When this happens, the pursuit of justice based on need is fulfilled.

The importance of this concept cannot be understated. The lack of understanding the difference between positions and interests is the root of all polarized issues and conflicts. This is true in interpersonal relationships, in the workplace, and in our faith communities. Churches and faith communities tend to be more prone to focusing on positions above interests. When the only focus is on the position without exploring interests, divisions occur.

Preparation

Interests and values are most often discovered during preparation. There are two components to preparation: tools and skills. Tools allow facilitators to gauge how integrated each participant is into their emotions and their understanding of the impact of the harm done to them. Tools also help determine a participant's readiness to engage in a restorative justice process. Skills refer to the skills facilitators need to help people prepare for the restorative justice process.

The more serious the harm, the more preparation is required. The goal of restorative justice is to make things as right as possible. The last thing that we want to do is create more harm. There are various ways to prepare participants using a variety of tools. These can include but are not limited to

- performing an initial assessment,
- taking a personal inventory,
- identifying support systems,
- utilizing role-play,
- creating questions and important statements, and
- writing letters to the other participant.

The initial assessment is a tool for the facilitator to gain insight into the lives of those impacted by the harm. This includes both the survivor and the one who did the harm. An initial assessment may consist of gathering more information on *family background*.

What were the important values in each family? Who in the families involved provides the most support in this process? What was the role of faith in each family? Understanding *interpersonal relationships* is also helpful in initial assessments. Which relationships have been impacted by the harm? How does each participant prefer to interact with others? Are the participants introverts, extroverts, or a combination? How do participants make decisions? And finally, exploring the *feelings* of the participants can be helpful. What are the reasons for each wanting to participate? What are their feelings about the outcome of the process? How does each participant deal with stress? What are the most significant issues or concerns of each participant?

Taking a personal inventory is different from performing the initial assessment and goes into more detail about the crime or conflict. It explores how the crime or conflict has impacted each participant. This tool can provide two essential elements in the process. One is to gain insight into the grief or loss of the participants, and the second is to give everyone the all-important opportunities for narrative. Remember the power of direct voice in chapter 1; this tool is a means to create the narrative. A personal inventory should begin with the story of the crime, event, or conflict. Other information may be gathered by asking questions such as

- What are triggers? What kinds of situations (sights, sounds, smells, events) trigger unpleasant reactions?
- Has anyone or anything been helpful to you? If so, what?
- Are you concerned the process could be harmful? If so, in what way?
- Were your relationships affected by what happened? How are those relationships now?
- Has the crime affected your lifestyle? If so, how?
- Has the crime affected your belief system? If so, how?

- What has been the worst part of this crime or conflict for you?
- What things would be difficult to hear from the person who harmed you?
- What do you think could provide the greatest sense of healing and justice?

Answers to questions like these will provide insight into the participants' values. First, the answers can help determine participants' readiness and possible expectations of interactions. The answers can help identify the motivation for wanting to participate. And finally, this assessment helps determine how integrated participants are in understanding their emotions and values.

It is helpful to identify what types of support the participants have. This support could include people outside the process that support participants, people to support participants in the actual process, and any resources the participants can access.

Role-play and prediction activities are valuable preparation skills used by a facilitator. Role-play can be done by asking participants questions based on specific things the other person may say. Some examples are:

- What will you do if the other person gets angry?
- How will you react if the other person shows no emotions at all?
- What will you do if you feel the other person is being dishonest?

These are just a few examples. The list could be endless depending on the nature of the harm committed.

Another valuable tool in preparation is creating a list of questions to be asked and important statements that need to be made. The last thing we want to see happen is a participant going into the process and regretting a forgotten critical question. Restorative justice processes can be highly emotional. Intense emotions can affect cognitive functioning. Emotions are internal noises that can hinder the communication process. It is common to see afterward how participants forgot things said during the process.

Another preparation tool is writing a letter to the other participant. The letter does not need to be shared or read to the other person, but it could be in some situations. Writing a letter forces participants to think about what is important to tell the other person. It is also a helpful tool for identifying thinking errors, which is more commonly seen in the one who has committed the crime. For example, participants may agree to participate and take responsibility but insert thinking errors like justifying, making excuses, or minimizing. When reviewing the letter, these errors can be pointed out. Then role-play and predictions can take place based on the error, like, "What do you think the other person will think when they hear 'insert thinking error'?" Or "How do you think the other person will react to the 'insert thinking error'?"

Denial

Clara attributes her suicide attempts to what happened to her as a child on the one hand and her father's denial on the other hand. She also acknowledges that his denial played a part in her anger and rage that affected not only her but also Tony and her children. It was his denial, more than the physical assaults, that led Clara down the path of searching for justice and to the eventual path of participating in Making It Right. She explained, "His denial felt like his way of intensifying the power he had, his way to make sure I continued to suffer and feel his power long into the future." So, when Thomas took full responsibility for the harm he did to his daughter, she knew she wanted—no, *needed*—to have access to that power and healing.

Not only is accountability a good thing that is required to facilitate reconciliation, but the absence of accountability has excellent potential to allow continued victimization or harm. Denial is toxic and cancerous and creates a ripple effect. The rippling effects of denial can be seen as it continues to affect Clara far into the future. When denial occurs, the natural human instinct is to erect an emotional wall to protect us from future harm.

There are a variety of forms of denial and each can be harmful. The first is the outright denial like Clara's father. It is the refusal to take responsibility and tell the truth.

Another form of denial is the belief that only "evil people" commit crimes, not regular people like our neighbors. The refusal to take responsibility is rampant in our churches and workplaces. An excellent example of this is the crimes of Larry Nassar, a doctor for the USA gymnastics team. Nassar pleaded guilty to sexually abusing ten minors in 2018. Currently, he is serving 40–175 years in a Florida prison for these crimes and sixty years for child pornography. In his role, Nassar molested hundreds of girls over decades. Looking closely, we see how victim blaming and denial played a role in allowing him free rein to molest children for years. Friends and neighbors of Nassar described him as a nice guy. Many predators like Nassar and Clara's father are "normal people" and, in some cases, even outstanding citizens in the community. People think someone normal or upstanding could never commit such a heinous crime. This is indicated in statements like "Joe Good could never do what he is accused of; he is a kind and generous person." This dangerous form of denial allows harm to run rampant.

A culture of sexual violence is perpetuated when people live in denial of the fact that bad things can happen to innocent people. Many people want to believe that society is fundamentally safe and if something bad happens, it's the victim's fault as much as the attacker's fault. This story comforts people into believing that they themselves will never be hurt because they do all the right things.

In 2018, the Mississippi *Clarion Ledger* wrote an article about a woman who was sexually assaulted while walking on a bridge used for exercise and the social media responses to that event. Many comments blamed the victim. Some comments were, "Too many people take too many risks. . . . No reason to put yourself in that position." And, "I would not run alone that late at night, especially being a woman. Go during daylight or go with a running buddy."[1] Comments like those above indicate we need our perceptions to be accurate so we can remain safe and make sure nothing bad happens.

Clara shared the story of a conversation with a woman in a small study group at her church. The topic of victims of sexual assault came up, and the woman shared her opinion that when sexual violence occurs, the issue is sin. The shocker was she was not referring to the sin of the offender. She meant the victims live in some form of sin that opens them up to a sexual assault. She explained why it is crucial to live a life focusing on the good, which motivates her to want to live out her faith. Statements like that translate to, "If it is not the victim's fault, and it was a random crime that happened to the victim, it could also happen to me." Fear says it must be her fault. It's easier to believe somehow, she was at fault; "She wasn't safe or good enough. I won't do what she did," or "I will be good and safe."

Denial creates the potential for secondary harm or pain. The first source of pain comes from the harmful act. The second source of pain comes from denial that anything wrong was done. Many emotions can rise out of that denial, raising questions like, Why won't they admit they are wrong? Why would anyone want to hurt someone like that? or even Why are they still being so mean? When we are hurt by someone else, as soon as the action occurs, it becomes a "past" event. It may have current repercussions, but the original harm is a "past" event that needs to be righted. Remember Matthew 5:23–24? "Therefore, if you are offering your gift at the altar and there remember that your brother or sister has something against you, leave your gift there in front of the altar. First, go and be reconciled to them; then come and offer your gift." That passage refers to a specific event or act that occurred in the past. It requires that amends be made, a "now" process.

Denial is different. Denial is both a "past" and "now" issue. Continuing to deny a harmful act from the past creates new harmful actions in the present. Denial is a second source of pain and can be equally harmful as the original offense because it continues indefinitely. Just take a moment to stop and think of a time when someone did or said something very hurtful to you and refused to take responsibility. Which was more painful, the initial hurt or denial that they did anything wrong? And, more importantly, where are you now in your relationship with that person?

It would be cruel to facilitate a dialogue between two people when the one who did harm denied it occurred. A conversation without personal responsibility and accountability can reestablish that original power imbalance and create harm from the ongoing denial.

A great place to start addressing the denial issue begins on a personal level. What level of personal accountability is in your life currently? Is personal responsibility for harm a value in your family, workplace, institutions, or church? If not, what needs to be done to bring this value to the forefront?

CHAPTER 4

Facing Fear

Note: The content of this chapter may be difficult for some readers and may cause triggers for those who have suffered similar crimes like Clara. The narrative in this chapter of Clara's story is deeply emotional and challenging. If you think her story may be too difficult to read, skip past the story to the concepts and restorative justice content. Otherwise, please continue with care.

The needle tracked on the vinyl record, mixing the lyrics with wispy sounds from scratches made by years of playing over and over. The song was a favorite from her time in college when she was deeply depressed. Somehow the notes seemed to capture her sorrow and hopelessness. In her hand, she held the note she had written years earlier. The note she left her friends after her third suicide attempt. The words seem to belong with the notes floating around her room. "My life is a mess. I need to confess, but all I want is to stop the wheels from turning. I know I should try, but I echo the lie that life is not worth the living. Tell everyone that I am sorry. But I can't go on, the pain is too much."

Tonight, she was not contemplating taking her life like she had when she wrote that note ten years earlier. Thankfully she was past that season in her life. Now, she had so much to live for: a wonderful husband, beautiful children, and a perfect job. But the bad was always present, even with all the good she had. The simple act of placing a needle on the record to hear the notes of a long-ago song took her right back to the darkness, the sorrow, the unbelievable pain. Tomorrow she would face a monster. Tonight, she remembered the pain, and the song's words touched that deep sorrow.

Last month, Clara finished all the preparations with Edward, the mediator assigned to her case, and the meeting with Thomas was scheduled for tomorrow. Her tan, muscular legs were crossed where she sat on the soft velvety comforter of her bed—laid out around her all the things she would take to the mediation, including this suicide note she had saved and her list of questions. She also had a small black-and-white photo of nine-year-old Clara where the shadows on her tiny face screamed to the world that this was a sad, lonely child. Next to the picture was a book she wrote and illustrated years ago as a young girl. The title of the book was *The Monster under My Bed*. The book tells the story of a frightened girl and how she survived dark nights living with a monster, detailing her nightly ritual.

> There's a monster living under my bed.
> My father says he's all in my head,
> but there's really a monster under my bed.
>
> He's the scariest monster I've ever seen.
> He's spotty and speckled
> and ugly and freckled.
> He's slimy and yucky and green.
>
> He won't come out by the light of day.
> He stays hidden and silently lurking
> until the moment the lights go out
> and his monster hands go searching.

To dodge this beast is not that hard.
It's really a simple trick:
Stand at the door and get ready to run—
but you must be clever and quick.

Turn out the lights, take a flying leap,
pull the covers up over your head.
For the monster can grab only the kids
that lie on top of the bed.

When the covers are up, count slowly to ten
and whatever you do, don't budge.
Don't poke your head out just one second sooner
or he'll gobble you up like fudge.

There's really a monster under my bed.
My father says he's all in my head.
But he's not in my head.
He's under my bed
and I hope someday he'll move.

Somehow that little book had become her standing stone. It was the evidence of the horrible nights when her father slinked into her room. Nights that on the following day he denied were real. Even as a child, she was trying to tell the world, screaming that bad things had happened in her house. But they were screams that fell on deaf ears.

Next to the book was the doll she made by hand when she was eleven years old. It was one of many toys piled in her bed every night as a child. She remembered how she gathered all her dolls and stuffed animals every night and set them up as sentries around the perimeter of her twin bed. The gray and white poodle, aptly named Grayie, stood guard on her pillow. Her father may have denied those nights in her room were real, but the army of poodles, bears, and dolls was a witness to the truth.

The doll was her favorite of them all. However, sleeping with the doll throughout her childhood had taken its toll. The brown knots embroidered on her cheeks for freckles were now unbound threads. A tiny hole in the flesh-colored cloth sat perched beneath one eye as if to become a permanent record of the tears wept. Her head forever flopped to one side since the stuffing in her neck was long gone. Stains dotted the yellow farm dress and white apron outlined in red rickrack.

There was no stopping the tears flowing this night as she stared at the doll. She felt like her little doll, tattered and worn, and oh, so tired. It felt like some great hand had plucked her worn-out self from her everyday life and tossed her on a conveyor belt. The belt was going toward the meeting tomorrow. She had no idea how she got on it and knew there was no way to get off. She felt as if she was helplessly moving toward something unfathomable.

Clara sent an email to several friends earlier that afternoon. They were the only ones who knew about the meeting other than Tony. They could be trusted completely. Their connection occurred years before when she was invited to attend youth camp at her church as an adult counselor. Her role was to provide support to the teens assigned to her bunk. She went thinking she was going to help the youth in her church. Little did she know that God had other plans. Each night, all the counselors met to discuss the day and how things were affecting them personally. Clara mentioned how moved she was by their willingness to open up and share their darkest secrets. As the evening meeting ended, the youth pastor Dennis and another counselor and his wife asked Clara if she was willing to share more about her comment. Before she knew it, she was telling them about her father. When she finished sharing, Dennis asked her how the abuse affected her relationship with God.

At first she was a bit caught off guard, but then to her own surprise she said, "Well, I know I can trust God as my savior, my lord, my helper and so much more. But there is no way I can trust God as my father."

"Do you want it to be that way?" Dennis asked.

After a few minutes Clara replied softly, "Not really."

The four of them began to pray. At one point Dennis asked Clara to think of the young girl who first experienced the horror of her past. A black-and-white image of the very sad Clara standing in her front yard for an Easter picture came to mind. The same picture lying on her bed. She wore a sweet white dress and shiny white shoes, but her stringy hair framed a face of hollow eyes and missing smiles. As she was seeing the image, Dennis gently took her hand and said, "How about we put her here" as he touched her palm. In her mind's eye Clara could do just that, she could see the little girl in the palm of her hand.

He continued with saying, "Can you imagine handing her to her Father God?"

When he said that, Clara immediately clenched her hand closed. There was no way. Dennis asked why she was afraid to let her go. Clara knew immediately. She opened her eyes, looking at the others in the small group and through tears said, "I can't. I am afraid he will reject me like my father did. I can survive what my father did, but if God did the same, I mean, he is God. What would I have. Who would I be but a nobody that even God rejected?"

The group asked if they could pray for her to have the strength to try and she agreed. After a few minutes of them praying, Clara realized she had to let go, she had to trust God. She felt like Peter when he said, "but Lord, where would I go. You alone have the words of eternal life" (cf. John 6:68). And with that realization she opened her hand. Again in her mind's eye she was that gray little girl standing in the palm of her hand but ahead of her was a glorious light that Clara knew was her Father God, she saw the young girl running, and as she did, all the gray began to melt off and golden flecks began to emerge. Within an instant Clara saw her younger self with golden hair and freckles dotting a face full of joy running into her Father's arms. There was nothing to do but weep in the presence of so much love.

Now five years later she was reaching out to those same friends to help her navigate the next scary step. The email she sent read:

> I know you're meeting with our small group tomorrow. Would you have the whole group pray for me tomorrow? I know this is going to sound strange, but here goes. I have told only the three of you about the surrogate mediation I am doing tomorrow. Not because I don't want them to know, but I didn't want any "cliché" comments or "pat" answers. I didn't want any input at all. However, tomorrow, when you ask the group to pray, will you be specific? Don't just ask them to pray for me because I am in a difficult meeting or whatever. I would ask that you ask them to pray for me because I am a victim of child rape and I am mediating with an offender who has agreed to be a surrogate in the place of my abuser who never admitted guilt. The surrogate was convicted of sexually abusing his daughter.

She needed them to know what was happening because she needed real prayers. She ended the email with:

> I need real fervent prayers because I am so scared. This is so real. The monsters are bigger than I am, and I don't know how I will face them and live. Please pray. Love Clara
>
> P.S. I think if a person could die of fear, I might die tomorrow.

Element #5: Safe/Structured Environment

In the email, Clara said, "I think if a person could die of fear, I might die tomorrow." The next day she would indeed meet with Thomas and face those fears. While she described feeling like she was on a conveyor belt and couldn't get off, in reality, she could. It was her choice to meet with Thomas. So, what would make someone experiencing fear to the point of death go ahead and step into that space? The answer is the restorative justice principle of a safe/structured environment. *Safe* is a tricky word. What does it mean because what feels safe for one person may not feel safe for another? In a restorative justice context, *safe* means creating a space with enough structure and support that allows people to enter in and face fears around challenging issues of conversations.

One victim shared how terrified she was by what she was about to do. She didn't "feel" safe. She was walking into a prison, which can inherently feel unsafe. And in a few minutes, she would be sitting a few feet away from the person who had harmed her most in her life. So feeling safe was not a part of the process. But elements in place made it as safe as possible for her to enter that prison anyway.

As a restorative justice practitioner, a major pet peeve is hearing someone say their goal is for their church or organization to be a safe place. The question that should follow is, What are you doing to make it safe? Simply wanting something to be safe or feel safe does not make it become a reality. So how do we create safe/structured environments?

The first thing required is *structure*. In restorative justice processes like victim-offender dialogue, there are specific guidelines to follow. The guidelines are the policies, goals, and preparation activities. In circles, as discussed in chapter 1, the structure is found in the use of a talking piece, the presence of circle keepers, guidelines, opening and closing ceremonies, and even in how decisions are made by consensus. Next, there are steps to process. While the content in each dialogue will vary, the steps in the process remain the same, and what becomes necessary is for facilitators to remember to trust the process. It is the process that keeps participants safe and allows for authentic dialogue, healing, and restoration.

Willingness is vital to creating safe/structured environments. The maximum amount of voluntary cooperation and minimum coercion is helpful since healing and relationships are voluntary and cooperative. Willingness can also be developed and strengthened by the facilitator in the preparation process. This is done by reminding participants they willingly sought out the process but can also stop if desired. This may sound simplistic, but someone considering stepping into a painful memory and discussing a traumatic issue needs to be reminded they have the freedom to walk away. Knowing that is an option is comforting and safe.

Openness is another way to create safe/structured environments. It may seem challenging to be open where there has been significant harm, but it happens all the time in the restorative justice process. The place to begin developing openness is in preparation. It is most effectively done by allowing participants to share without judgment. This can be modeled in two ways. One way is demonstrating your willingness to communicate openly. And another is asking questions that promote openness.

Another element of safe/structured environments is *respect*. It can be specifically named and often follows guidelines like "In the circle, we will speak with respect" or "In the circle, we listen with respect." Listening is more than waiting for your turn to speak. When listening respectfully, we give our full attention to the speaker and the heart behind the words. Participants can also be reassured that if the atmosphere becomes disrespectful, it is the responsibility of the facilitator to address the issue and help the group reestablish a respectful space. Leaders and facilitators must model respect.

Dignity is another component of creating a safe/structured environment. Dignity is provided in the most simplistic form through direct voice for all participants. Dignity can be a challenge for survivors. No one would ever say to a survivor, "Now remember you need to treat the offender with dignity." But the reality is there is inherent dignity in every person created in the image of God. It is even found in those who commit the most heinous crimes like rape and sexual assault. We see that in Clara's story. She hated her father for what he did to her. But she loved her father as well. She saw the inherent dignity in him despite what he did. Another woman who was also a victim of child sexual assault by her father said she never wanted her father to go to prison. She only wanted him to stop what he was doing to her. Thomas knew he could walk into a space and allow Clara to spew all of her rage because he knew Edward saw his inherent dignity.

And finally, to create safe/structured environments, it is also important to examine issues that can hinder that safety like microaggressions, unhealthy silence, and bias.

Microaggressions

It is important to understand the concept of microaggressions when creating a safe/structured environment. Microaggressions are indirect, subtle, or unintentional discriminatory statements or actions, against members of a marginalized group such as women or a racial or ethnic minority. The presence of microaggressions indicates a culture that can perpetuate sexual harassment and sexual violence. Two steps need to be taken to eliminate microaggressions: first, provide training to employees, managers, and leaders on the issue, and second, point out when a microaggression occurs and take necessary steps to address it. Below are a few examples of microaggressions that can be directed toward women, BIPOC people, and the LGBTQIA community:

- Asking someone where they are really from. This implies they are not American.
- Labeling assertive women as bossy or a bitch, while describing assertive men as strong leaders. This form of microaggression implies women are out of line if they are confident or assertive.
- Saying I don't see color. This denies a person of color's racial or ethnic experiences; not to mention, it is completely illogical.
- Asking the woman in a meeting to take notes instead of a male counterpart. This assumes that secretarial tasks should be a woman's responsibility.
- Clutching a purse when a person of color approaches. This communicates to them, "I think you are a criminal."
- Following a person of color around a store. By doing so, the salesperson is communicating, "You are here to steal."

In 2014, *I, Too Am Harvard* was released. According to the website it is "A photo campaign highlighting the faces and voices of black students at Harvard College. Our voices often go unheard on this campus, our experiences are devalued, our presence is questioned—this project is our way of speaking back, of claiming this campus, of standing up to say: We are here."[1] In the photo campaign individual students held up signs of microaggressions they encountered. Below are just a few.

No. I will not teach you how to "twerk."
Don't you wish you were white like the rest of us? —old friend
You're LUCKY to be black . . . so easy to get into college." —old classmate
Oh, I heard her say she was going to Harvard. I just assumed she misspoke. —white parent to my mother

You don't sound black . . . You sound smart.
You're the Whitest Black person I know.

Microaggressions like these, left unaddressed, will destroy safe/structured environments.

Silence

Silence is a powerful means of communication. There are times when we need to speak up and times to remain silent. Sadly, in many contexts, we have the use of silence mixed up. Being silent when hearing someone voice a microaggression is all too common. When someone voices a microaggression, that is the time to speak up. When someone is sharing difficulties or pain around sexual violence, that is the time to remain silent as it is a wonderful way to support and allow them time to express what is important.

When it comes to dismantling toxic cultures, understanding and identifying reasons people are silent is necessary. Too often we dangerously assume that silence is a sign of agreement. That may not always be the case. There are other reasons people will remain silent, including

- thinking about a situation or what was said;
- feeling minimized;
- lacking confidence or fearing retaliation for speaking up;
- having differing views from dominant voices; and, most dangerously,
- recognizing an imbalance of power in dialogue.

If we are serious about changing our culture, we need to recognize the dangers in neglecting silenced voices. From a restorative justice perspective neglecting silenced voices goes against the goal of dialogue and the element of direct voice. Not addressing silence due to unhealthy reasons mentioned above further excludes, oppresses, and minimizes individuals and diminishes an individual's humanity.

There are strategies for addressing those unhealthy silences. The best strategy is to ask questions of others, first about their typical responses to disagreements and issues of race/power/exclusion. If silence is a response, explore what needs to be present for them to feel safe to speak up. Asking people questions about preferred communication styles is also helpful. Some people are simply shy and prefer not to speak up that much. In this case, silence is a preferred communication style and not necessarily unhealthy.

When silence does occur, asking simple questions for clarification is a good starting point. This is best done one-on-one. Even if you are in a group setting and you realize one or more individuals are silent on a topic, it may be necessary to take a break and check with each person individually. It can be as simple as asking, "I noticed you were silent in our conversation. I just thought I would check to make sure things are okay." If you are still uncertain, a follow-up question could be, "Would you be willing to share your thoughts about the topic?" However, if you are the individual's supervisor, in a higher leadership role, or in the majority either by gender or ethnicity, it would be better to have someone on the same level, gender, or ethnicity as the silent participants to ask the above questions.

Identifying Bias

Finally, as a facilitator it is critical to examine bias in the context of creating a safe/structured environment. We all bring bias into relationships and dialogue. Ignoring bias is foolish and can destroy the feeling of safety for others. Below are a few questions that can be a good starting place.

- How are the issues of gender and sexual violence recognized or not recognized in our church, organization, or workplace?
- What additional resources do we need before engaging in dialogue around the issues of sexual violence? (Do not assume that you have all the insight you need.)
- How do power and privilege impact our culture and workplace?
- If we come from a different culture, how may our own assumptions and perceived roles contribute to further harm?

When addressing the topic of sexual violence some questions that can help with bias are:

- What is my personal and institutional power?
- What are my points of access?
- What systemic things need to change?
- What am I willing to do personally, as a church, organization, or company?

Fear

There is a close bond between power and fear. Fear is an underlying motivator in the quest for power. The more fear a person has, the more they will seek power and attempt to control every aspect of their environment.

Clara shared during preparation for her meeting with Thomas that the details in the children's book she wrote were her actual nightly ritual. The unpredictability of the visits from Clara's father created a need in her to control as much of her environment as possible as a child. From her childlike attempt to "escape the monster" to the sentinel of stuffed animals posted in her bed. Survivors of any form of sexual violence know all too well the significance of fear.

But fear, while it may be an unpleasant experience, is not always a bad thing. Imagine walking down a beautiful country lane, and suddenly you hear soft rattling and see the tail of a giant rattlesnake in front of you. Fear should stop you in your tracks. Fear will direct you to slowly back away and, when possible, run in the other direction. There are times in Clara's story, as there often are with other survivors, when fear plays a valuable role. For example, in chapter 1 of Clara's story, when Clara closed her eyes, her father became angry and more violent. After that event, it was because of her fear of making her father angry and making things worse that Clara did what she was told. In that situation, fear protected Clara from something worse.

But more importantly, fear can be overcome. Psalm 23 is a beautiful illustration of overcoming fear.

> The LORD is my shepherd,
> I will not be in need.
> He lets me lie down in green pastures;
> He leads me beside quiet waters.
> He restores my soul;
> He guides me in the paths of righteousness
> For the sake of His name.
> Even though I walk through the valley of the shadow of
>   death,
> I fear no evil, for You are with me;
> Your rod and Your staff, they comfort me.
> You prepare a table before me in the presence of my ene-
>   mies. (NASB)

Clara loved this psalm because her whole life was living in the shadow of death, but somehow, in spite of that knowledge and the fear she once felt, she also knew God would lead her once again.

Every act of sexual violence is different, and every victim who survives will do so in the only way they know how in the moment. Some survivors chose not to resist out of fear of death or greater harm. This instinct may be the very thing that keeps them alive. But sadly, it can also become a point of contention and self-blame. Multiple rape victims who have participated in victim-offender dialogue have shared the struggle of questioning whether they did the right thing by following this instinct. So what can we do to help survivors as they process the experience of fear?

Most states have victim-offender dialogue programs to allow victims of violent crime to meet with their offenders in prison or on parole. So, what role can the church and other organizations play in assisting survivors of rape and sexual assault? A starting place would be to assess your organization's or church's current culture. Do all the principles required to create a safe/structured environment exist? If not, what can be done to make those changes?

One of the most beneficial outcomes of restorative justice processes like victim-offender dialogue and circles is the diminishment of fear. One example is a woman who wanted to meet with the man who raped her. When she met her mediator at the front gate of the prison, she breathed in rapid, shallow breaths. As she pulled her driver's license out, her fingers trembled so badly that she shoved the license in the slot for the guard, then quickly crammed her hands in her pockets to hide her fear. After checking them in, the guard opened the large metal gate for them to enter the prison. Walking the long sidewalk from the outer gate to the prison's interior took much longer than usual. The victim's steps were small and sluggish. She walked with her head and shoulders down. She would take a deep breath every so often and let it out slowly. As they got to the room where the meeting was to take place, she sat stiffly at a small picnic table in the visitation room.

She turned to her mediator and shared how nervous and scared she was. Her mediator checked to ensure that she still wanted to continue and reassured her they could leave if this was more than she had expected. She said she knew this would be hard but didn't realize how hard it really was. But, she also said, she had to continue.

The meeting went remarkably well. She confronted her attacker, challenged him, and in the end forgave him. They went through all the formalities of closing the process and preparing to leave. Then, she and her mediator began to walk down that same long sidewalk from the prison's interior to the outer gate, the same sidewalk she inched her way across earlier that morning. As they walked that afternoon, the sun was high in the sky and a gentle breeze blew. After only a few steps back out, the victim began to skip. And she skipped, *literally* skipped like a little girl, back to the guard gate. Why the dramatic change? The simple answer is that she faced her fear; she faced her greatest fear and survived. The freedom she found in that revelation was to celebrate and skip to her new future.

PART 2

The Who

CHAPTER 5

Moving Forward

Rage filled her mind as she dug her fingernails into his flesh. With all her might, she sought to dig her fingers into his eyes and gouge them out. Then, just as she was about to accomplish her goal, she bolted awake. When she did, she realized it had been a dream. Staring into the dark room, she thought of the first time she met Thomas, and he shared his shame of sexually assaulting his ten-year-old daughter. Her first reaction to his words was the dream tonight. But, when he took responsibility for what he had done, Clara remembered how she felt two things at the same time. She remembered wanting to gouge his eyes out as in her dream, but she also remembered wanting to kiss him on the cheek. She wasn't sure which behavior was the sickest.

The first time she heard Thomas speak weeks ago set her on this journey of participating in Making It Right. To participate in Making It Right, the victim must initiate the process. Once Clara contacted the program, she was assigned a mediator, and the case was opened. After attending the first meeting and learning all about the process and policies, her mediator, Edward, contacted Thomas to see if he would be willing to participate.

Edward met with Thomas and explained that the process was voluntary. He explained that Clara's father committed a similar crime and was never convicted, never admitted guilt, and had since passed away. Thomas was familiar with victim-offender dialogue because he participated in one with his daughter. The process had been profoundly healing for both father and daughter. Meeting with Clara would be his third mediation and second surrogate mediation.

As soon as Edward left the meeting with Thomas, he called Clara and told her he had agreed to participate in the mediation. Clara was pleased but also perplexed that he had. She thought, *Why would he agree to meet with me? He has never done anything to me. Why would he put himself in a position to be called a monster by someone he has never met? Did he see himself as a monster?* She considered her father a monster and hated him. But she also loved him. She hated that fact—that she both hated and loved her father.

She didn't even know Thomas. So, she couldn't hate him, but in a way, she did. *Why would he sit across the table from me, a stranger, and allow me to vent my anger and hate about something he didn't even do to me?* she wondered. She had no clue why he agreed, but she was grateful he did. The knowledge that Thomas decided to meet with her meant this was real. Was she ready to look back into the trash pile of her past and dig up the ugliness? Her husband thought she was crazy. He did not understand how meeting someone who had never hurt her would help. But Clara was used to being called crazy. She waffled back and forth, believing it herself, and asking herself, *Am I really crazy? Or am I the sane one and my father the crazy one?*

Clara and Edward worked together for the next few months preparing for the meeting. They met once a month for several hours. Edward would ask questions and talk about possible scenarios for the meeting. He also gave her assignments. For example, one assignment was a ten-page personal inventory about how the crime her father committed affected her, both then and now. There was so much to think about, and so many emotions stirred up in the process.

During this preparation phase, a friend suggested she participate in a spiritual retreat. A weekend retreat might be perfect timing to help her sort out her feelings and thoughts. Tony thought it was a great idea too, since he, once again, was clueless how to help. He thought the one thing he could do was support her by keeping the kids while she attended. Unfortunately, the retreat rules did not allow participants to have cars or cell phones with them while at the retreat. After Clara's friend dropped her off at the retreat and drove off, panic set in. Clara felt trapped with no way to escape. She tried to calm her nerves by reminding herself that this was a Christian retreat. But her heart would not listen.

There were about twenty participants at the retreat and about ten women hosts. There were sessions every morning and afternoon where someone spoke about different aspects of faith and living as a believer. Half the time, Clara didn't hear the speaker's words because she could not shake the panic of being trapped in this place. She hated when she was not in control. The retreat center was about twenty miles from town, and she seriously considered walking to town to find someone to call her husband to pick her up.

During a break, Clara went to a side porch to try to calm herself down. Not only was she panicked about being here, but she was also constantly thinking of the upcoming mediation, adding fear on top of fear. Fear of meeting and talking about what her father did. On top of that, talking about it to a stranger. Not just any stranger, but a monster stranger. But was he a monster if he did something so noble and kind for her? Her mind was rambling. She had to figure this out. She had to calm herself down. There had to be a reason all this was happening.

She decided she was not going back in for the next session. She sat on the swing, the breeze feeling sweet against her cheeks. She needed space to think and figure out why she was in such a tizzy.

Clara loved to memorize Scripture. She memorized Psalm 91 and prayed it during times of stress like this: "He is my refuge and my fortress; My God, in Him I will trust" (Ps. 91:2 NKJV).

As she began to pray, a host came up and interrupted her thoughts, "It's time for the next session to begin, so if you would please rejoin the group."

Annoyed at the interruption, Clara turned and said, "I am not going in for this next session. I need some time to think and pray."

The woman said, "You don't understand. You have to participate in all the sessions."

Clara's annoyance turned to anger, and she spat out, "No, you don't understand; I am not going back in, so get the hell away from me and leave me alone!"

The host's cheeks turned bright red. She looked like she was tripping over something as she stumbled backward and rushed back into the center. Clara was alone with her panic and fear again. She went back to praying Psalm 91 to help her calm down.

> He who dwells in the secret place of the Most High
> Shall abide under the shadow of the Almighty.
> I will say of the LORD, "He is my refuge and my fortress;
> My God, in Him I will trust."
> Surely He shall deliver you from the snare of the fowler.
>
> (Ps. 91:1–3a NKJV)

But then she stopped with the sudden realization of the words she had just prayed,

> Surely He shall deliver you from the snare of the fowler.

It hit her like a ton of bricks, and she cried out to God, *But you didn't!*

She prayed the rest of the scripture, every so often adding her reply.

> And from the perilous pestilence.
> He shall cover you with His feathers,
> And under His wings you shall take refuge;
> His truth shall be your shield and buckler.
> You shall not be afraid of the terror by night,

but she replied, *but I am.*

> Nor of the arrow that flies by day,
> Nor of the pestilence that walks in darkness,
> Nor of the destruction that lays waste at noonday.
> A thousand may fall at your side,
> And ten thousand at your right hand;
> But it shall not come near you.

But it did.

> Only with your eyes shall you look,
> And see the reward of the wicked.

It was not just with my eyes. Is this my reward? And am I the wicked?

> Because you have made the LORD, who is my refuge,
> Even the Most High, your dwelling place,
> No evil shall befall you,
> Nor shall any plague come near your dwelling;

but it did, it lived in mine.

For He shall give His angels charge over you,
To keep you in all your ways.
In their hands, they shall bear you up,
Lest you dash your foot against a stone. (Ps. 91:3b–12 NKJV)

But they didn't, and it crushed my soul.

Clara was completely caught off guard by the thoughts she inserted in her prayer of this scripture. Who was she to question God? Who was she to challenge what Scripture said? Yet, for the first time, she questioned the Scriptures. If God didn't do what he said he would do in this scripture, does that mean it is not true? Or does it mean she does not belong to God? Part of her was so angry at God that he didn't do what this word said he would do; another part was ashamed.

There was a question on the personal inventory that Edward gave her that she didn't answer. The question was, "Has the crime/loss affected your belief system? If yes, please explain." When she read that question initially, she wasn't sure how to answer. She always wondered why God allowed that to happen to her, but she wasn't sure it affected her belief system. She still went to church. Of course, she fell away from the church in her teens and college years when she was on her rampages. But even then, she still believed in God. She hadn't answered the question because she wasn't sure it had, that was, until this afternoon.

Dragging her toes in the dirt forced the swing to stop. Everything stopped. At that moment, she realized her anger toward God. He did not do what he said he would do! It was as if nature reacted to that knowledge. No cool breeze relieved the heat of angry blood rushing to her cheeks. No leaves rustled to distract her mind from such heresy. But worse than the anger was the thought that followed. If God didn't do what he said he would do, he must not love me.

With that realization, she crumpled on the swing and wept.

Impact of Sexual Violence

While there are many shared experiences in the aftermath of sexual assault, it is essential to remember that each person will process the devastation individually. There is no one way to react after an assault. Therefore, it is necessary to give survivors autonomy to navigate the days afterward. Some common responses immediately following an assault are shock, disbelief, numbness, dissociation, shame, embarrassment, anger, anxiety, depression, and denial.

In my years working with victims of sexual assault through victim-offender dialogue, I heard many victims describe these early days with comments like, "It felt like this can't be happening to me," "This can't be real," or "This must be a nightmare, and I just can't wake up."

Violent crimes disrupt belief systems. They violate a person's basic assumption about how the world works. As a result, they can create a loss of control and trust. This is evident in Clara's story. From early childhood, her views of how the world works dramatically shifted and continued into adulthood.

The long-term effects in Clara's story included anger, rage, self-destructive behaviors, the use of alcohol and drugs, mental instability, depression, and promiscuity. Clara became promiscuous very early. It would seem that someone who experienced the trauma of child sexual assault, as Clara did, would want to avoid any close intimate relationships that could remind them or trigger thoughts of what happened. And while that is true for some, it isn't for others. Because the sexual behavior attracted Clara's father to her, she believed her value was tied to those sexual acts. If her father wanted her for sexual reasons, she must be attractive to him. So, she also felt it was true for all the men she was with in the past.

Sexual assault is a crime of isolation that can lead to, as Clara experienced, depression and thoughts of suicide. Survivors of sexual assault experience isolation for a variety of reasons such as personal shame, victim blaming, fear of not being believed, self-blame, and embarrassment. According to studies gathered by the Rape, Abuse & Incest National Network (RAINN), "the likelihood that a person suffers suicidal or depressive thoughts increases after sexual violence."[1] Consider the following statistics:[2]

- Post-traumatic stress disorder (PTSD) affects nearly all women who are victims of rape with 94 percent experiencing PTSD within two weeks of the rape.[3]
- Of those women affected with PTSD, 30 percent continue to experience symptoms nine months later.[4]
- Following rape, 33 percent of women contemplate suicide, while 13 percent of them actually attempt suicide.[5]
- Studies show that 70 percent of victims of rape or sexual assault (a higher percentage than victims of other violent crimes) experience some degree of distress.[6]

In 2008, Debbie Smith was a part of a video series with the Office of Victims of Crime. In that video she details the after-effects of sexual violence.

> I went into immediate shock. I was like a zombie. This can't have really happened to me. I've got to be dreaming and I just can't wake up. I couldn't sleep. When I did finally sleep, there were nightmares. I couldn't eat. I couldn't think. I couldn't focus. A lot of people told me after I was attacked, "Debbie, at least you're alive." And I remember thinking, *I am not alive.*[7]

Debbie's words reflect the experiences of many. But the reality is while there is some commonality of reactions after an attack, each victim's experiences are unique to them.

Triggers are another after-effect of sexual violence. Triggers are some form of stimulus that causes painful memories and emotions to resurface. Often triggers can bring back the same intense emotions the survivor felt during the attack. Examples can be the crime's anniversary, media coverage of similar events, a similar trauma, holidays or significant life events, and even smells associated with the crime. One survivor explained that the pain never goes away, "It's like that it lays just beneath the skin waiting to be touched. When it is, the wound is just as raw and painful as it was in the beginning." This is not to say that life can't get better. It can and has for many. But the mind and the body do not forget the trauma. How to navigate that trauma and pain when it rears its ugly head must be learned.

Clara shared during her preparation how isolated she felt as a child. Her fear and shame made it challenging to function in school, and she explained she had very few friends growing up. When she was very young, her only close relationship was with a cousin of a similar age. The words she used to describe herself were "sad and lonely." She explained that not only is that how she described herself, but it became her identity. It was an identity that led to dramatic mood swings of depression and suicidal thoughts, and suicide attempts.

Cognitive Dissonance

Human beings are meaning-making machines. We are constantly seeking the meaning of our everyday experiences. Survivors are no different. In the disruptive aftermath of a violent crime like sexual violence, survivors will eventually arrive at a place of trying to understand what happened. Some will question why this happened to them. Meaning-making is extremely difficult in the context of violent crime. Trying to make meaning out of something inherently meaningless is a challenge.

To understand and create spaces for healing for survivors of sexual violence, it is critical to understand the concepts of ambivalence and cognitive dissonance. The terms are similar in definition, and both are prevalent in survivors post-trauma. According to the Merriam-Webster Collegiate Dictionary, ambivalence is "simultaneous and contradictory attitudes or feelings (such as attraction and repulsion) toward an object, person, or action."[8] And the definition of cognitive dissonance is "psychological conflict resulting from incongruous beliefs and attitudes held simultaneously."[9]

Both of these concepts are seen in Clara upon hearing Thomas speak. She both hated and loved Thomas at the same time. She wanted to both attack him and kiss him. The presence of both emotions is ambivalence. The internal conflict she struggled with in experiencing both feelings simultaneously is the psychological conflict of dissonance. Clara didn't understand how she could feel both emotions at the same time.

Contradictory emotions are common among many victims of violent crime. Another example is found in a Julie Speers video production released in 2011 of a woman named Sandy that chronicles her family's journey through a restorative mediation with the young man who killed her son in a DWI accident. At the end of the mediation, Sandy states, "I would hate to even imagine where I'd be physically and mentally if we hadn't gone through this restorative mediation. It was just like we were reborn." But then she adds, "the pain will never go away for my son. I love him, and I cry every day."[10] On the one hand, she was reborn physically and emotionally. On the other, the pain will never go away. The truth is that both realities exist at the same time.

The opposite of this ambivalence or dissonance is binary thinking; either/or, right or wrong, good and bad. There is a place for that thinking, and it is good in some contexts. Some survivors have experienced difficulty in relationships due to binary thinking. A woman sexually assaulted by her father as a child shared how her husband's binary thinking caused marriage problems for years. She said, "He simply could not understand how I could forgive my father and still want him in my life after surviving such horror by him."

What she heard was *if he did something this horrible, he was a terrible person, and nothing good could come from future interactions with him.* For years, she felt something must be wrong with her because, on the one hand, the husband was correct. Her father was a horrible person for what he did to her. So why would she want to be around him? Because she still wanted a relationship with her father and sought to meet with him in a victim-offender dialogue. It was a healing process; afterward, she realized it was okay to interact with her father. She beautifully explained it by saying, "What he did to me as a child left a hole in my heart. If I went through life without a father, it would create another hole in my heart in the absence of my dad. If I forgive him, I have a father and only one empty place in my life." She chose forgiveness and a relationship with careful boundaries about future interactions. This situation is not to promote that survivors should seek relationships with those who hurt them. It simply reveals the danger that binary thinking can come across as judgment against the survivor for the ambivalent or dissonant emotions experienced in the aftermath.

When restorative justice processes are used, opportunities for healing and finding healthy boundaries are possible. In 2006 the documentary *Beyond Conviction* highlighted the stories of three victims that participated in victim-offender dialogues.[11] One of the participants was a young woman whose mother was murdered by her boyfriend. After the incredible, forgiving, and healing process, the victim stated, "I don't feel like I am talking to an enemy." But she added, "I don't feel that I could ever have tea or nothing with you. But, like I said, I don't hate you at all."

Outsiders may not understand all the survivors' experiences. What is essential is the willingness to accept that everything may not always be black and white. And more importantly, support survivors and ensure that they know when ambivalent or conflicting emotions occur, it is okay to feel what they need to feel.

Active Listening

The greatest gift we can provide survivors is a listening ear. Sadly, for the most part, people are terrible listeners. While most are poor listeners, it is easy to understand why. We are taught how to speak from a young age. We learn communication skills in school through reading, writing, and even a few classes like public speaking. However, listening is not a skill that is typically taught in most schools. It is as if it is an inherent skill we assume everyone has, but in reality, most don't. But we can learn to become better listeners.

Active listening has two purposes in creating a sacred healing space for survivors. The first purpose is to listen for interests. What are the values, interests, or needs behind the words victims share through communication or on the assessments or role-plays? The second is to engage the participants in the process. How well we listen determines how much people will reveal the complex, intimate issues inherent in sexual crimes.

So, how do we become active listeners? Facial expressions can indicate we are listening. If someone is talking about something sad, our facial expressions may become somber to reflect that message. In doing so, the person speaking can visually see that we hear their message.

Posture can indicate listening. Leaning in when people talk communicates we are interested in what is being said. Crossed arms or a body position turned away from someone when they are speaking sends the message we are not interested or not listening, even if we are.

We can encourage people and validate what they share to show interest and to keep them talking. Sometimes it helps to restate what someone says to confirm the facts by telling them in a slightly different way. Reframing is another tool similar to restating in that we repeat what someone says but also include the underlying message or interest. An example of reframing could be, "I heard you say you were angry, but it also sounded like there was sadness."

And finally, active listening includes clarifying by asking appropriate questions to gain an understanding of the issue that needs to be resolved. This could be a question like, "Could I ask a few questions to clarify in my mind?" Then, go on to detail possible interests or values that need to be addressed. Learning to become an active listener is a skill we can continually improve. We can always be better listeners.

CHAPTER 6

Choosing Words Wisely

Could you see past her eyes? As soon as she wrote the question, Clara began her mental self-abuse; *what a stupid question to ask. You can't ask that of a perfect stranger. If you ask that question, they will think you are losing it.* Yet, despite all her negative mental slams, she could not bring herself to erase that first question in her journal. And just as quickly, she wrote a second question. *Could you see inside her soul?*

Clara met earlier that morning with Edward, and her assignment was to write down all the questions she wanted to ask Thomas. They could be questions she wanted to ask her father but couldn't. Or they could be questions about Thomas, his crime, and his life. Clara took the assignment as a reason to buy a new journal. Clara loved journals. So much so it was almost an obsession. She began journaling in middle school and never stopped. As soon as Clara filled one journal, she bought the next.

When Edward left that morning, Clara jumped into the car to head to the mall. The assignment he just gave her to start writing her questions and thoughts deserved its own journal. The words that would fill those pages didn't need to be mixed with the words of her everyday life, didn't need to and didn't dare. Oddly, the journal she picked for the task was about as plain as you can get. It was a simple brown cover with a slight snakeskin texture.

Back home, sitting in her favorite spot to think and write, she opened the new book and wrote those first two questions. Could you see past her eyes? Could you see inside her soul? But it was more as if the questions wrote themselves because Clara was caught entirely off guard by the words. She wanted to erase the words but could not bring herself to do it. There was something about those twelve words that demanded an answer.

As Clara stared at the page, she noticed the slight twitching in her fingers. She remembered those nights in her room when her father stared at her face. She hated that he stared at her so closely. One night she closed her eyes, and her father went ballistic. Immediately, she felt the pressure of his thumb gouging into one cheek while all four other fingers dug into her other cheek. He squeezed so hard her mouth was forced open.

Her father hissed, "Open your eyes!"

Quickly obeying, she saw his clenched teeth between twisted lips and deep furrows between his eyebrows. It was pure rage on the face of the man who was supposed to love and care for her.

He whispered through his clenched teeth, "Don't you ever shut your eyes. Do you understand?"

When Clara didn't answer quickly enough, his fingers dug deeper into her cheeks as he said each word as if it were its own sentence. "Do. You. Understand?"

Through her still tightly squeezed duck lips, she softly replied, "Yes."

She never closed her eyes again. When Clara woke up the following morning, five purple splotches were on her face. One perfectly round splotch on one cheek and four interconnected splotches on the other. As soon as her father saw her, he said she would not go to school and he would call the teacher. After breakfast, he made a sandwich, put it in the refrigerator, and told her she could have it for lunch. Then he left for work. He went to work and left his eight-year-old daughter with splotchy cheeks home alone.

After he left, Clara sat at the dining room table for over an hour, afraid to move. What was she supposed to do all day? Was this a test? Was he going to come home and find her doing something fun and get mad? Was she supposed to sit here all day till he came back? If it weren't for the fact she had to go to the bathroom and was about to wet her pants, she might have sat in that chair all day. But nature called, and she went to the bathroom. When she came out of the bathroom, she saw some stuffed animals on her bed were now on the floor. So she walked into her bedroom and snatched them up. For the next few hours, she arranged and re-arranged the animals around her bed, sweetly talking to each one when she picked it up.

Now sitting in her home with her new journal, thinking about that day, Clara wrote a third question. *Didn't you see the toys in her bed?* And the fourth question quickly followed, *Didn't you see that she was a child?* Of course, she knew many other questions to ask, but those first four were the ones that mattered most.

As Clara remembered that day and the night before, she knew why those first two questions wrote themselves on the page. They had always been there. As she reread them, the tears began. *Oh, dear Lord, please let the answer be no.* Her deepest fear was the an-swer was yes. Why else would he stare into her eyes? It was as if he wanted to see past her skin and into the secret places in her heart. The private place where a little girl's innocence is stored. Where little girl dreams are kept safe. She feared that his penetrating eyes wanted to see into those secret places to steal and destroy what was never his to touch.

Shaking her head, Clara decided that was enough for one day. This process was not what she expected when she started this jour-ney. She didn't know what to expect, but it sure wasn't this. The thoughts and memories in this process could catch her off guard. But she also knew there was no way she could stop. But for now, she needed a break.

It was her day off, and she needed to get things done. So, she put the journal away, grabbed her keys, and, as she headed out the door, her phone rang. It was her friend Katy. Katy knew it was her day off and asked if she wanted to go to lunch. Clara was already thinking about lunch, so she quickly agreed. They met at their favorite bistro and ordered their typical soup and sandwiches. While waiting for their food, Clara told Katy about her meeting with Edward and her assignment.

Katy was one of the few people who knew Clara was preparing to meet with Thomas. She also knew what Clara's father had done. Clara didn't tell Katy about her four questions. She wasn't even sure she could speak them out loud. But she told Katy it was hard to think about what to ask, especially since Thomas never really did anything to hurt her. She explained that she was afraid she would say something hurtful. Katy reassured her she wouldn't.

But Clara said, "Yeah, well, you wouldn't believe some of the things people said to me."

She went on to tell Katy that she learned the hard way years ago to be careful who she told, like that night in high school when she heard the disgust in the voice of her friend Emily when she said, "Your own father?"

She also told Katy the second person she trusted with her secret was an old boyfriend, Steve. They had been dating for several months, and things were starting to get serious. One night after they had been partying, Clara told Steve about her father.

He commented about that being pretty intense, but then followed with the question, "Why didn't you tell him to stop?"

She thought about it for a minute, but then was livid and said, "For real? Are you kidding me? I was five years old."

Needless to say, the relationship didn't last.

"Wow," Katy said, "I am sorry you had to hear that."

Clara shrugged it off. They finished lunch, and Clara finished running her errands. When she got home, she returned to her room and opened the journal again. Reading the four questions, she knew they were the right questions. Even if Thomas had no idea how to answer them, she knew they needed to be asked.

Words Matter

The average person will speak around seven thousand words a day. How many of those seven thousand words are carefully selected? How many are even given a second thought? For the most part, people don't think about the words they speak. We only realize when the wrong words are spoken, and someone else reacts negatively. They are a huge part of our everyday life. Yet, most of the time, we throw them about thoughtlessly. How often do we think about them, how we use them, what they mean, and their power? But if we want to learn how to create sacred spaces for healing for survivors of sexual violence, we have to start at the beginning, and that is understanding that our words matter. How we string them together can make all the difference in conversations and relationships. But words brought healing to the victims we have read about in previous chapters. Words exchanged with the one who should have been the enemy. Words from the enemy brought new life. Words are important.

Words matter to God. The power of words is rooted in Scripture, found in the very beginning of chapter 1 of Genesis. God could have created our world any way he wanted, but he chose words. "And God said, 'Let there be light,' and there was light" (Gen. 1:3). It is not enough to see that words were spoken and something was created. It is essential to know the power behind it. God saying, "'Let there be light,' and there was light," reveals that words become the source of power. Where there was once nothing, there is now something because of the spoken word.

The first verse in the New Testament proclaims the importance of words. "In the beginning was the Word, and the Word was with God, and the Word was God" (John 1:1). Words are so important that "Word" is the first name in the New Testament to describe the Son of God. While many people never think about words and their power, the Word did.

Christ is also called a mediator:

> For there is one God and one mediator between God and mankind, the man Christ Jesus. (1 Tim. 2:5)

> For this reason Christ is the mediator of a new covenant, that those who are called may receive the promised eternal inheritance—now that he has died as a ransom to set them free from the sins committed under the first covenant. (Heb. 9:15)

Throughout Scripture, we can see how beautifully he plays the role of the mediator, connecting those he encounters in his ministry with his Father. In Scripture, Christ spoke to individuals in different situations to make those connections. We can live out that Christlike attribute in our day-to-day lives. In restorative justice, dialogue words are the foundation to move us to create spaces for healing and accountability as individuals, businesses, churches, or organizations. The more we learn to wield the power of our words for the good of society, the better our world will be. The more we understand and discover the power of words when working with survivors, the more prepared we will be to bring healing.

Questions

Questions are an essential part of restorative justice dialogue. In everyday life, we use questions all the time. Yet, like words, we don't often think about the quality of our questions. The following line from David Whyte's poem "Sometimes" is the profound truth: "questions that can make or unmake a life."[1] Questions will either bring greater understanding and draw people together, or create confusion and harm and push people farther apart. Asking questions can accomplish many things. Questions can help us gain information about a particular issue, clarify and determine which issues are most important, help us understand different points of view, identify feelings and values, and help others understand their needs and interests. Asking questions is essential in restorative justice processes. There are two things to consider when asking questions: the types of questions to ask and the actual words within the question.

Types of Questions

The types of questions one asks will either facilitate or inhibit the restorative justice process. Two types of questions that enable dialogue are *open-ended questions* and *direct questions*. Open-ended questions can provide information, expansion, and clarification on a topic. Open-ended questions do not elicit a "yes/no" answer but rather begin with the words *what*, *who*, *how*, *when*, or *where*. Open-ended questions are used when there is a need to gather the most information about a particular topic or issue. Asking questions like, How does your family celebrate the holidays? can provide many details.

Direct questions, however, tend to elicit a yes/no or one-word response. They don't reveal a lot of detail, but they do provide clarity and help keep things flowing. Direct questions offer a specific answer and can help in clarifying issues. In addition, because they focus the discussion and narrow the possible reactions, direct questions are helpful in equalizing time in conversations. For example, if one person tends to talk more than others in the group, it may be necessary to ask a direct question of that person to minimize their response.

There are also two types of questions that inhibit dialogue and may cause defensiveness: *leading questions* and *"why" questions*. Leading questions imply an answer and may give the impression the person asking them is taking a side. This type of question can create defensiveness in people. Leading questions should be avoided in conflict dialogue and when discussing polarizing issues or when working with survivors. If you ask questions like, Don't you think that idea is fair? you will appear to be siding with the one who made the suggestion.

"Why" questions should be avoided in conflict dialogue, when discussing polarizing issues, or when there has been harm. When you ask someone a "why" question, you are asking them to defend their position; defensiveness is never helpful when resolving conflicts or problems or when developing relationships needed to engage in effective dialogue. When people are defensive, they may shut down or become combative, neither of which is useful in challenging conversations. They can also sound like cross-examinations and cause people to become more defensive or suspicious.

While asking "why" questions is not good in certain situations, the information the answers would provide could be valuable in those situations. To get the relevant information needed without making people feel defensive or suspicious, reword the "why" question so that it becomes an open-ended question. For example,

Why did you do that?
becomes
What led that to happen?

Why didn't you tell her?
becomes
What was your biggest concern in telling her?

Why do you feel that way?
becomes
What might have led to those feelings?

Why not?
becomes
What would be a better plan?

Making these modifications may seem silly, but it always works.

Wording of Questions

The words we choose in our questions can make a difference. The English language is full of innuendo and can be easily misinterpreted. Our English language also contains biased words that can cause defensiveness or carry negative messages. Using neutral language is a practical tool to help guard against negative messages or statements. Using neutral language can de-escalate tense situations, support people in communicating, and solve problems more effectively. In addition, people who use neutral language and reframe the discussion as such are less likely to be perceived as siding with one person or another or having a personal opinion about another person's behaviors, views, or attitudes. The best way to neutralize language is to remove words that create defensiveness, adverse reactions and emotions, and polarization. The negative words need to be replaced with more neutral ones while still conveying the same meaning that the negative ones convey.

Christ also demonstrated the skill of neutrality in how he spoke to some people like the woman at the well in John 4:17–18. Christ knew the truth about the woman's life. But look carefully at the language he used with her. He asked her to go and get her husband.

She replied, "I have no husband."

He responded, "You are right when you say you have no husband. The fact is, you have had five husbands, and the man you now have is not your husband. What you have just said is quite true."

What Jesus said is a neutral way of saying, "Of course not, because you are an adulterer." His choice of words allowed him to confront the sin in her life but do so in a way that she still maintained her dignity and was open to continued dialogue. In that continued dialogue is found the fullness of reconciliation. Look at the response of the woman in verses 28 and 29: "Then, leaving her water jar, the woman went back to the town and said to the people, 'Come, see a man who told me everything I ever did. Could this be the Messiah?'"

Not only did she recognize the truth he spoke, but she also went on to tell others about him. It is also a beautiful example of the power of neutral language.

Let's look at a few examples of neutralizing questions. For example, someone may ask, Do you think he is lying? The word in that question that has the potential to cause defensiveness is "lying." To make the question more neutral and avoid defensiveness, it could be changed to, Do you feel he is being honest? The meaning stays the same, questioning the truth of the situation, but the negative word "lying" is replaced with the more positive word "honest."

Another example could be a question like, Do you feel she is untrustworthy? The negative word in that question is "untrustworthy." To neutralize, change the question to, How reliable or responsible do you think she is?

The most common mistake with asking neutral questions is taking the negative word out altogether and not replacing it with something neutral. In the examples above, that would look like, What do you think about her?, or, How do you feel about her? However, there are two problems with that approach. The first problem comes in the answer to a question like that; you are inviting a negative response. For example, you ask, How do you feel about him?, and the response will likely be a negative statement like, I think he is a liar.

The second problem with just removing the negative word is that it changes the specificity of the dialogue. If lying is the issue that must be addressed, removing that word keeps from addressing a critical value. The ultimate goal of neutral questions is to replace negative words while maintaining the meaning or topic that needs to be addressed.

Neutral language seems logical and straightforward enough, but in reality, it is counterintuitive. It is not our natural way of communicating, and it takes practice. A thesaurus is an excellent way to increase proficiency in neutral language and aid in asking more neutral questions. Look up synonyms of negative words and choose one that has less sting but keeps the original meaning.

When people are brought together to have a dialogue or conversation around emotionally challenging topics like sexual violence, the individuals likely will not be using neutral language. The facilitator helping with the discussion must know how to reframe those negative statements or questions into neutral ones to de-escalate potential defensiveness and adverse reactions. Neutral language can help plan the actual questions the facilitator may ask in the dialogue. A good facilitator will ask neutral questions that still get at the heart of the issue.

At times, neutrality requires that we temporarily suspend judgment of the people in the process or temporarily suspend judgment of what needs to be the outcome of the process. In this time of suspended judgment, interests are identified, common ground can be identified, and people begin to view each other differently. Temporarily suspending judgment allows us to see the humanness of everyone, even the one considered the "enemy."

Realizing each other's humanness, dignity, and interests can drastically change predetermined positions, judgments, and solutions the people had before coming into the process. Our first reaction to someone who has harmed us is to judge. And there is a place and time for that. But if we want to create sacred space for survivors of sexual violence, temporarily suspending judgment is necessary. It is also a very biblical concept. Christ is the ultimate example of suspended judgment. He suspended judgment to see our humanness and dignity, enter into a relationship with us, and love us. He suspended judgment and took our sins on himself to allow us to enter into a relationship with him. It is the basis of that relationship, and that relationship alone, that reconciles us to God. Of course, there will be a time when we will have to account for our actions. But there was first a time when grace was offered.

A powerful example of asking the right questions while temporarily suspending judgment can be found in the story of a young man convicted of brutally beating, raping, and murdering a young college student. He agreed to meet with the sister of the victim for mediation. During preparation, the man was very concerned the sister would call him a monster for what he did. He was willing to take responsibility, but he hated the idea that people might think he was some monster.

In preparation, he shared with his mediator that he lived in the same apartment complex as the victim. So one day, he followed the woman, and as she opened the door to her apartment, he grabbed her and shoved her inside, where he violently beat, raped, and killed her. When he finished, he went back to his apartment. He could see her apartment from his, and the next day he realized no one was checking on her; no one had called the police. So that night, he returned to her apartment to steal her television and other valuables.

As he told the mediator about returning to the apartment, the mediator asked the man, "Where was the victim when you returned to the apartment?"

The man replied, "She was still on the bed."

The mediator asked, "What were you feeling when you saw her on the bed?"

"Nothing," he said, "I didn't feel anything."

The mediator paused and let that response hang for a moment, and then asked, "What are you feeling or thinking right now as you tell me what happened?"

Slowly shaking his head, he said, "That I sound like a cold-hearted monster."

Neutral questions with suspended judgment led him to choose the word he most hated, *monster*, to describe himself. The mediator could have used the term *monster* in preparation because his actions were heinous. But instead, he trusted the process and used the correct tools. As a result, the truth was discovered, allowing for a powerful meeting to follow weeks later, where the victim's sister offered the repentant man forgiveness.

CHAPTER 7

Understanding Power

Focus, Clara, focus! Clara slowly sucked in a breath and held if for a few seconds before exhaling. Edward sat in his chair in the center of the five-foot-long oak table as he explained the ground rules for the mediation. Thomas sat on his right at the end of the small table. And Clara sat on his left, forced to stare at the man who was and was not her monster. Her large tote bag was on the floor holding all the items from the night before, neatly packed, each waiting to emerge as testimony to years of sorrow.

Edward explained they would begin with an opening statement from each of them, one or two sentences about what each one hoped to gain today. Clara would go first.

"I am not really sure what to expect. Mainly because you're not the person who injured me," was all she had to say.

Thomas replied, "It's okay. I hope you find some answers today even if I am not the person who hurt you."

Edward's nod to Clara was his invitation for her to start the day. Clara fumbled through her tote and pulled out the papers with her past writings and the small journal with all her questions. She began by reading a journal entry she wrote years before.

There is a black hole in the midst of my soul. It takes my breath away in the night. I've hurt so deeply for so long. Life seems to slip away at the time it should be the fullest. I cannot believe I was created to be a person with part of my soul missing. God, where is the rest of my soul? Where have you hid it? Please, Father give it back to me. I know it was once here. I want it back.

Laying the pages back on the table, Clara explained this was why she was here today. Her hope that maybe today would be the day she would be whole again. For the next few minutes, Clara explained her current life. She shared she had a wonderful husband, beautiful children, and a job she loved. But even with all the good there was this void inside that always reminded her she was not whole, that she was broken and unworthy. She also told Thomas of the time she confronted her father and how he denied doing anything to her.

Thomas listened intently and when Clara stopped, he asked, "How can I help you today?"

"Well, like I said, I am not sure. What would you like me to know about you?"

It was now Thomas's turn to take in a deep breath and slowly exhale. He began. It started when his wife passed away in a car wreck. He was left to raise their two daughters on his own. He clarified that the death of his wife was in no way an excuse for what he did, it was just the "how" of all that followed. His daughter Kelly was twelve and her younger sister was nine. He went on to say a few months after his wife died he began grooming Kelly. He would have her make a grocery list and drop her off at the store to do the household shopping. He was trying to make her take on some of his wife's daily tasks. Multiple times he referenced his twisted thoughts and thinking errors that allowed him to do what he was doing.

"The power of denial is a perverse power, an ugly beast," Thomas explained.

It was his denial that allowed him to begin grooming Kelly and eventually led to him molesting her over the course of several months. That ugly beast of denial is a strong animal that is not easily fought off. Thomas said the best weapon he has to fight it is to feel the pain of what his actions caused. Meeting with Clara this day was a way to better understand and, more importantly, feel the pain and trauma his actions caused.

After a few months Kelly finally made an outcry to a close friend and he was arrested. In the beginning he denied it all and blamed Kelly for making up lies. There was no way he was going to admit what he did. He would lose everything and possibly face prison time. A meeting with his attorney convinced him that his chance of acquittal was slim, if not impossible. Eventually, he admitted his guilt. He was placed on probation and was prohibited from any contact with his daughter. Kelly and her sister went to live with their aunt. It was his admission of his guilt that allowed him to begin the journey of owning all that he had done. The truth was that he committed the crime and traumatized his daughter. His denial wanted to reverse those roles.

After he finished, Clara wasn't sure what to ask next so she opened the journal and began. The first few questions she asked were fairly innocuous. What was your daughter like? How old was she when you committed the crime? But then she moved to a question that was harder to ask. Did you dislike her afterward? When Clara wrote that question, she already had an answer she expected to hear, and Thomas did not disappoint by answering, yes, he did. Clara lost it and couldn't stop tears from flowing.

He explained in his twisted thinking he was angry at her for making him want her. He was the one who traumatized her and yet he was angry at her. But then he quickly added that he never hated her or thought she was ugly or disgusting afterward. Clara responded, "I knew that was the real truth and the sad thing is that the pain of what he did isn't the worst part. The worst part is that he no longer approved of me."

After all he had done to her, Clara still wanted approval from her father. After all *both* of her parents had done, she still loved them. If only her father had been like Thomas and given her the gift of the truth. If only he had taken responsibility and admitted what he did. Every time he denied what he did was like screaming to Clara, "You are not worthy of the truth. You are not good enough."

Clara looked at her journal and told Thomas the only questions left were the ones she didn't know if she wanted to ask, to which he quickly responded, "Remember, I chose to be here."

When he said that Clara's immediate thought was that he was warning her to be careful about what she was about to ask and not be too mean or demanding on him. But she was wrong. He went on to explain that it was his choice to be in this room and nothing she wanted to ask would offend him. Clara was caught off guard. He was giving her free rein to be as brutally honest as she needed. This was almost too much. How could someone who did such horrible things be so kind? They decided to break and return to the questions after lunch.

The time away at lunch allowed Clara to gather her resolve and ask the questions, "What did her eyes look like?" and "Could you see past her eyes?" She was about to clarify with "not the color or anything." Thomas quickly responded asking for clarification if she meant during the times of abuse or all the time. His interruption was unbelievable. To her his question meant he knew exactly what she was asking. He knew exactly what she needed to know.

She responded, "Both."

Thomas explained when she wasn't being abused her eyes were sad and lonely. Clara was caught off guard when he explained that most of the time during the abuse, she had no eyes because he refused to look at her. But he added, the few times he looked at her, the answer was yes, he could see past her eyes. Clara knew it. She just knew it. For years she felt as if what her father did gave him the power to see past the surface of her eyes. Knowing the last question would be the hardest, she asked, "Do you feel as if you could see into her soul?"

Immediately he responded, "Yes. I felt like I had all the power and I could devour her soul."

Clara was undone. Edward and Thomas sat silent as she sobbed tears that deserved to be wept from the question that deserved to be asked. Once she composed herself, Edward asked Clara if she was angry with her father. She said she was not. Thomas was caught off guard and asked where her anger was directed. Clara shared about the weekend retreat and her prayer of Psalm 91. She was angry at God. Where was he? Why didn't he save her? She was unable to trust God because he had not been there for her. And if she did try to trust him again and he let her down again, she might not survive.

Eventually, all of her questions were asked. Edward asked if they wanted to make any type of affirmations or requests for each other based on what they experienced today. Thomas went first and again thanked Clara for all she shared. Knowing her trauma, understanding the trauma of his daughter, and feeling that pain was the only thing that helped him in his recovery and kept him from potentially harming again.

Clara reiterated her thanks for his willingness to meet with her in spite of the fact that he never did anything to hurt her. Timidly she asked Thomas, "The next time you see your daughter would you tell her, 'Everything will be all right and everything will be okay'? Because that is what I desperately wanted from my father."

Thomas agreed. "I know you're going to get where you need to be. It may not be with all the t's crossed and i's dotted, but you will get there. I see your strength."

Clara smiled. "You know I think I will, too. I have so much more hope today than I did before."

Power

The concept of power is absolutely fundamental to the restorative justice process. It is critical to understand power and its role in everyday life. Sexual violence is not a crime of passion, nor is it even sexual. Sexual violence is about power. It is coercive power to completely dominate another. Power is the ability for one individual to influence the actions of another individual through coercion, intimidation, threats, physical force, or harassment. Power is different from authority. A person with authority has inherent power that comes from the position granted or given to them. While a person with authority has power given to them, it can be abused. In fact, it is common that sexual abusers are often people with authority. These could be doctors, teachers, bosses, supervisors, coaches, caretakers, religious leaders, and parents.

Power occurs naturally throughout society. Parents have power over children, bosses have power over employees. Power in and of itself is not the issue. It is when power is abused that problems arise. Autonomy affects power. When people lack autonomy they are at greater risk of being manipulated and harmed by others. Economics also play a role in the power dynamic. The lower the autonomy and access to resources, the lower the power.

If we want to create sacred space for survivors of sexual violence, power structures and imbalances must be addressed. And any real conversations around the issues of sexual violence will and should include those who have power and those who do not. It is completely possible to have healthy dialogue with people of power in the room as long as there is an intentionality to balance the power in the process of the dialogue.

Power can be used for good or for evil. Thomas misused and abused his power with his daughter. Then he used his power for good when he met with Clara. He had the power to say, "No, I will not participate in a surrogate mediation." But he said yes. Like words, power shows up very early in the Bible. In Genesis, Adam and Eve are created in the image of God. Genesis 1:26 says, "Then God said, 'Let us make mankind in our image, in our likeness, so that they may rule over the fish in the sea and the birds in the sky, over the livestock and all the wild animals, and over all the creatures that move along the ground.'" Power is revealed in two ways in this scripture. The first, man is created in the image of God, in his likeness. If we are created by the all-powerful, we inherit power. The purpose of the power we inherit is seen in this scripture: humans are to "rule over the fish in the sea and the birds in the sky, over the livestock and all the wild animals, and over all the creatures that move along the ground." It goes even further in verse 28 to say, "God blessed them and said to them, 'Be fruitful and increase in number; fill the earth and subdue it. Rule over the fish in the sea and the birds in the sky and over every living creature that moves on the ground.'" God blessed them, he blessed them both, man and woman. He gave them both, man and woman, power to rule over the earth and the living creatures. There is no mention of man and woman being given power over each other or other future humans. That misuse of power came with the fall when they chose to sin and use the power God gave them to be disobedient to God.

There is no coincidence that power and words are right there in the beginning of Scripture. God very clearly pairs the two concepts together in the creation story. Remember, the very first concept of restorative justice detailed in chapter 1 is direct voice. God knew the voice was our greatest source of power. Our words carry power to others, either for good or for evil. But more importantly, our voice is how we identify ourselves, how we reveal ourselves to the world. We choose words to tell others who we are: a mother, a father, a sister, a child, a lover, or a fighter. It is not an accident that perpetrators of crimes of sexual violence seek to silence those who are harmed. Clara's father told her every time he came to her to be silent and tell no one. The man who raped Debbie Smith (see chapter 5) told her not to tell anyone or he would come back and kill her. Abusers threaten and demand silence. They use power in an attempt to silence those who have been harmed.

Power and words are right there at the beginning. Crime and violence are the very first story of man. This is why the first chapters in Genesis point directly to the biblical need of restorative justice. It is a call that power must be restored, that voice be given back to those like Abel whose blood cries from the ground for justice. It points to the expectation to make things right by returning voice and power to the voiceless and powerless; that is true justice.

Abusing Power

Power is abused in many ways. It happens when someone uses power to forcibly harm another. It happens when someone uses power and threatens or coerces another. It also happens when those in authority and power do not use their authority to protect others and look the other way. An excellent example of the last abuse of power is the case of Robert Shiflet, the junior high youth pastor at Denton Bible Church in Denton, TX, who was convicted on federal charges of sex trafficking minors across state lines. Reports of inappropriate behavior began in the 1990s, but it wasn't until 2019 when the accusations became public that the church launched an investigation. The report was written in 2022 and said that in 2005, two of the victims reported the abuse to counselors and elders of the church. The only action those in authority and power took was to remove his ordination as a pastor. This action only has importance within the church setting. Those with power did not report the accusations of the victims to any outside authority.

The findings of the report illustrate a misuse of power. "The investigation revealed three broad areas where serious mistakes were made by Denton Bible leadership: (1) we did not protect these children from their youth pastor, (2) we did not have a victim-centered response, and (3) cultural dynamics at Denton Bible contributed to or exacerbated these failures."[1]

Even though the report issued by the elders acknowledges their failings, it is full of thinking errors. Each of the three areas of their serious mistakes are detailed further in the report. In the section where they "did not protect these children from their youth pastor" the thinking error of excuses is evident. "Twenty years ago, we were not prepared to recognize the warning signs of grooming behavior. Even though reports were made of inappropriate behavior by Shiflet, we did not understand the way predators groom their victims and gatekeepers."[2]

This case in Denton is one of the many that have come up over the years. It is this turning away by those in power that has fueled movements like #metoo and #churchtoo. What is important about the subsequent report on the crimes in Denton is that it is reactive. Nothing was done until reports were made public. If churches want to help prevent such crimes from occurring, they must be proactive. Churches and organizations must begin to implement policies and processes that both help prevent sexual violence and also provide support to those within who have experienced sexual violence.

Denial is the third way power is abused. And it's one of the themes that came up over and over and over in the preparation and surrogate mediation between Clara and Thomas—the impact of her father's denial of his abuse. Denial is a method the abuser used to continue to assert power and continue to abuse. During the mediation Clara made the statement, "You are not worthy of the truth. You are not good enough." The act of denial becomes a weapon that her father powerfully wielded. She also shared that she stopped asking her father to admit what he did because she didn't want to give him the power to hurt her every time he denied his crime.

As much as power can be misused it can be useful. If a child is about to run into the street into an oncoming car, a parent may use power to grab the child. Individuals with power in organizations and churches can use their power to deconstruct systems that create rape culture. They can also use their power or authority to create opportunities for healing and justice for survivors. What this may look like will be discussed more in chapter 9.

Regaining Power

There are a variety of ways to help survivors regain a sense of power including the many books and resources available to survivors that address the harm done through sexual violence. However, the path to regaining power is different for each person. Regaining power could be achieved through journal writing or exercising or changing hair styles or repeating empowering statements like, "I am stronger than I give myself credit." Having a support group can also be helpful. Begin with making a list of resources that might be beneficial: formal support groups, individual therapy, group therapy, and informal support groups. While friends and family can create one level of support, participating in support groups with others who have shared experiences can be very helpful.

Neglected resources that are highly effective are those used in restorative justice processes: victim-offender dialogue, surrogate mediations, and circles. In these processes power is restored in multiple ways, one of which is providing survivors a direct voice. A rape survivor once said, "I need to say to him, I'm not afraid of you anymore, you can't hurt me anymore." Words spoken to the one who did the harm can restore power that was taken through violence. Giving survivors a voice in the process helps them determine outcomes for harms done and allows them to articulate how the crime impacted their lives. This provides justice based on needs and pain. Again, it is important for each person to recognize how, when, and where to share their stories. Some survivors find it helpful to share their stories while others find it difficult. What is important is for each one to find what works best for them.

Tools to Balance Power

Restorative justice processes themselves balance power. The autonomy provided to the survivors, the use of a talking piece in circles, the search for values and needs, and the direct voice allowed to all participants are all methods that balance power. There are other skills or tools that help balance power as well. They are to avoid assumptions, articulate expectations, and provide intervention and support. These are used within various restorative justice processes, but they also apply in other contexts as well, as when addressing workplace conflict or family relationships.

Avoid Assumptions

We all do it. We all make assumptions. Allowing assumptions to go unchecked can create rape culture. A common assumption around sexual violence is that the victims somehow brought it on themselves. While it may be prevalent in society and, in some cases, even instinctive to make assumptions, we must take a step back and seek clarification. We can all think of a time when someone did something to hurt us or make us angry. If you are like most people, you have either had the thought or said out loud to someone, "I know what they are thinking" and then add your assumption. The truth is we cannot know what someone is thinking. The only way to know is to ask. Sometimes our assumptions are correct, but more often than not they are wrong.

Articulate Expectations

What can participants expect to get out of a dialogue or restorative justice process? If we want to have healthy dialogue around issues of sexual violence, we must ask about the expectations of each stakeholder coming into that space. We know from chapter 3 that preparation is important for creating space to provide healing for survivors. Determining expectations is useful in the early stages of preparation. Questions such as the following can help determine expectations: What do people hope to gain in the process? What are motivations for wanting to participate? What would you expect from those who disagree with you? What would you hope they would understand, or do? For those in power, how does your power play a role in this process?

Provide Intervention and Support

When it becomes evident that one person has less power than others in the group and those with power are trying to assert their power over that one, it may be necessary for someone facilitating dialogue to intervene. It is also helpful to provide support and encouragement to those with less power. During the preparation for victim-offender dialogue, the victim is in control the entire time. For the most part, the victim has complete autonomy and control of the process from beginning to end. Something as simple as allowing the one with less power the opportunity to speak first helps balance power.

CHAPTER 8

Forgiving Our Debtors

Numbness flooded Clara's body as she sat silently on the bed. It was over. She met with Thomas and survived. Clara knew the process was going to be difficult and worked it out with her family to take time away after the mediation. She made a reservation at her favorite hotel in the mountains. It was only a one-hour drive from where the mediation took place, and Clara assumed the drive to the hotel would be soothing with all the beautiful scenery on the way. But the truth is she didn't remember a single moment about the drive. It was as if she was in the mediation and then she was in the hotel sitting on the bed.

She had the luxury of time and used it to just sit in the silence and begin to process all that happened. Eventually the growling in her stomach stirred her to realize she had not eaten since breakfast. They took a lunch break during the mediation, but she just moved pieces of pasta around her plate because her nerves made it hard to swallow. Now famished, she thought to herself, *If there was ever a day I deserved room service, today is the day.* Glancing over the menu, Clara picked up the phone and ordered a steak and baked potato. She was going to order a glass of wine but opted for the entire bottle.

Thirty minutes later she devoured her meal and half of the wine. Thinking about the day, she wondered what it all meant.

Why had God taken me on this journey to relive the pain of my past? Why had he brought Thomas into my life? There had to be a reason for all of this. Sure, she had answers now that she hadn't had before. As she thought back over all that was said, she remembered something Edward asked her during the mediation. He asked if she was angry with her father. It struck her now that the question seemed to come from nowhere. They hadn't been talking about her anger. Edward asked that question right after Thomas answered her question affirming her fear that her father could see inside her soul. Was she supposed to be angry? Is that why he asked? But like she said in the meeting, she was not angry at her father, though she guessed she should be. All her anger was directed at God. Where had he been? Why hadn't he protected her? The more she thought about it, the more anger boiled up inside. She lay back on the bed allowing her anger to stir. She had a right to be angry. No one was there for her those horrible nights.

In her mind's eye, she saw that little Clara as her father walked out of her room one night. The tiny frail body lying still on the tossed sheets in the dark. Little Clara not daring to move until she was sure he was gone. Even after he was long gone, she lay still in the darkness unable to process with her six-year-old mind what was happening, why her father hurt her like he did.

As Clara saw that broken child lying completely alone in the dark she cried out to God, "Where were you? Why did you leave her all alone to face the monster, to be devoured by the monster?"

As soon as the thoughts hit her mind, it was as if someone said to her, "Look again." Not sure what the words meant, she knew to obey. She closed her eyes and once again it was like she was floating in the corner of the room looking down at her six-year-old self, lying alone in the dark. Look again? She moved her eyes around the empty room and when she did, she noticed a shadow moving in the corner. Then out of that shadow stepped who she instantly knew was Jesus. Slowly he moved toward the child on the bed and knelt beside her. It was then that Clara saw what looked like dirt on the little girl. With tenderness Jesus began to remove the filth. Once she was clean, he brushed a curl off her forehead before turning back to the shadow. Before he disappeared back in the corner, he turned to the Clara looking down on the scene. He whispered, "I was there. I was always there. She was never alone. I saw the sin and removed it and I will take it with me to Calvary." Then he was gone.

Instantly, Clara woke up with tears streaming down her cheeks into her ears. She must have fallen asleep after dinner. The dream was so real and so vivid; she remembered every detail. There was no stopping the tears that needed to be wept. She had not been alone. She replayed the scene over and over in her mind unable to fathom the power of its meaning. Jesus took the sin from those nights upon himself. He took it to the cross. That realization hit Clara like a bulldozer. If he was willing to bear that sin for her, she had no right to hold on to it any longer. As quickly as she realized that truth, she knew she must forgive her father. Ever since he denied hurting her, she could not bring herself to forgive him. If he could not be a man and be honest, he did not deserve her forgiveness. But this night she knew she must.

Still crying she spoke into the empty room, "Dad, I forgive you. Do you hear me? I forgive you, Dad. I forgive you and I love you."

As the words left her mouth, Clara lamented the fact that she would never have the opportunity to say those words directly to him. Her arms ached with the desire to hold her father one more time as she forgave him. But that touch would never be found. The words of forgiveness would forever drift like orange and red leaves on the fall wind, never finding a resting place.

Even though she was exhausted, she sat up. The lights were still on and she reached for her journal. It was important for her to remember the dream and write it down. When she opened the book, she read the last entry from the night before the mediation.

It was just the words, "Psalm 23." She couldn't remember why she wrote that scripture. Opening the drawer on the bedside table, she found and pulled out a simple black Bible. She flipped through the thin translucent pages to the book of Psalms. She grabbed her pen to write the words as a prayer, but hesitated. As she read the words, she realized it was the story of her past, a story to be remembered, a story to be documented. She wrote her own personal version of Psalm 23.

> So many tried to bring death to me.
> So many laid me down in the beds of lovers of hate.
> Their desire was to plunge a hole deep into my soul
>   so the life-giving water would forever fall through
>   the cracks like a broken cistern in a dry parched field.
> Each attempt on my body was another hammer to deepen
>   the broken
>   cracks in what was to become my crushed spirit.
> Numbly I was led to the bed of death to have my innocence
>   robbed over and over again until all that was left was
>   an emptiness that nothing in this world could fill.
> Then you came and picked up the pieces of my broken heart.
> You looked at the filthy bed in which I lay.
> My eyes cried out to you "Lord, heal me, please touch me."
>   "I know you hear my cry!"
> Gently you touched my bruised hand and lifted me from
>   the filth.
> You walked me beside a gently flowing stream.
> You sat me down in a place of peace.
> Your hand, the hand of a swift cutting physician,
>   meticulously cut away the death that was injected
>   through the
>   lovers of hate to eat away at my soul like a cancer.
> The clear waters purified your hands.

Then you led me back through the valley and right there in
    the midst of
      my enemies you sat me down on the bed where death
        tried to reside.
Right there in the darkest hollows you spread out a table
    before me to
      feast on your righteousness and holiness.
The eyes of the scorners and mockers raged at the sight
    of the restoration of my soul.
Continue to lead me past the darkness of my seeds to a full
    restoration
      so that the harvest of your kingdom in my life will be
        bountiful and
      produce the lovely fruit you chose me to produce.
How is it I fear no evil in these depths
. . . because thy rod and thy staff, they comfort me.

With that, she closed the book and turned out the light. It was done.

Forgiveness

In the context of sexual violence, or any violent crime for that matter, the concept of forgiveness is a touchy and complex subject. So many victims over the years have shared beautiful stories of forgiveness. And just as many have shared horror stories. Forgiveness is challenging on a daily basis with issues that come up between friends and families. Imagine how much more challenging it can be when associated with the trauma of sexual violence.

In April 2020 Everett L. Worthington Jr., PhD, published a white paper where he said, "One paradox that has been often noted is this. Most people highly value forgiveness. Religions advocate it. Talk-show hosts advise it. Yet, despite all this positive attention, most people struggle to forgive."[1] So, what does research say about forgiveness?

According to an article from the American Psychological Association, "Research has shown that forgiveness is linked to mental health outcomes such as reduced anxiety, depression and major psychiatric disorders, as well as with fewer physical health symptoms and lower mortality rates."[2] That article goes on to address another study done by Loren Toussaint, PhD, a professor at Luther College. In that study, "Toussaint followed participants for five weeks and measured how their levels of forgiveness ebbed and flowed. He found that when forgiveness rose, levels of stress went down. Reduced stress, in turn, led to a decrease in mental health symptoms."[3]

There are a variety of definitions of forgiveness, but most center around the concept of intentionally choosing to release feelings of resentment, anger, and vengeance toward someone who hurt you, regardless if they have asked or deserve it. We can forgive on a cognitive level and on an emotional level. Cognitively we think, *I no longer wish bad on the person who harmed me. I choose to release them from what they did*. Emotional forgiveness may be more challenging due to all the complex emotions associated with significant harm. It may even come up more than once when experiencing some trigger around the harm. When negative emotions come in again, there may be that sense of, *this is just not fair*. It can also happen when reliving all the negative emotions associated with trauma and recognizing the harm was not just in the past, but also present in the now with triggered emotional trauma and pain. Victims have shared how they forgave their offender but every so often something would trigger a memory and the anger and pain would reemerge along with the need to offer forgiveness again. Those who are able to do this are a beautiful example of what Jesus taught when Peter asked him about forgiveness: "Then Peter came to Jesus and asked, 'Lord, how many times shall I forgive my brother or sister who sins against me? Up to seven times?' Jesus answered, 'I tell you, not seven times, but seventy-seven times'" (Matt. 18:21–22). Seventy-seven times, in other words, we may find the need to offer forgiveness over and over unlimited times.

Forgiveness is not just an issue of faith. People outside the faith community recognize the need for forgiveness when wronged. We all want forgiveness when we are the one who hurts another. But we can struggle to offer it when we are the one who has been hurt. For some the ability to forgive comes naturally. Many survivors of violent crime offer forgiveness to the perpetrator early on in the process. One woman told the story of the night her daughter was violently beaten, raped, and left for dead. The night she got the call that her daughter was in ICU, as soon as she hung up the phone she prayed, "God I'll forgive whoever did this if you just let my daughter live." Her daughter did survive and the mother continues to forgive the man convicted of the crime.

For others the process is not as quick or as simple. In many cases, the more significant the harm, the more difficult it is to forgive. In an interview with ABC News after meeting with her attacker, Debbie Smith shared about forgiveness. When asked why she wanted to meet with her offender she replied:

> I get that question a lot. . . . The main reason was because with the women that I work with that have been sexually assaulted, I teach them about forgiveness. But I always have to say . . . that I don't know how I'd feel in front of him, but I think that I have done the work, and I do believe that I have forgiven him. And so I had to meet with him to know that that was true. In fact, before he said anything, before we got into a huge conversation about anything, that's what I led with. From what my advocate says, that's unusual, that's usually the end. But to me, if I had really forgiven him, then it couldn't depend on his actions or

his words, or his lack of words to me. It had to be regardless of his attitudes or words. Because to me that's what true forgiveness is . . . forgiveness is what happens in my heart.[4]

Debbie ended that meeting and shared with her husband, "I am finally free. I have no fear. It did more for me than the trial did."[5]

Clara was asked to speak at a victim-offender symposium about the concept of forgiveness. She shared the details of the night after the mediation and how she arrived at the place to forgive her father. She also shared other experiences around forgiveness. She sought out a friend at her church during a time she was struggling with issues involving her father's abuse. The friend suggested the reason she was still struggling with the negative emotion was due to the fact that she had not forgiven her father. The friend went on to say until she was ready to forgive, she would never get over what happened. The old "you need to forgive and forget" cliché. While it sounds good, it is completely unrealistic. Even if forgiveness is offered, there is no forgetting being sexually violated as a child for years. Suggesting it can be forgotten minimizes and dismisses the significance of the trauma. What Clara heard from her friend was it was her fault she was suffering. Her father harmed her, but because she chose not to forgive, she was choosing to suffer.

Clara struggled with the conversation and finally decided to reach out to her pastor in order to help her better understand forgiveness because she was not ready to forgive her father for what he did. During the meeting he read her the passage in Matthew 6:14: "For if you forgive other people when they sin against you, your heavenly Father will also forgive you." Her pastor went on to say, even if she did not feel like forgiving her father she had to do it or she would not be forgiven of her sins. She left the meeting even more discouraged because she was just not ready.

Probably her most significant moment around forgiveness came on a business trip to Fresno, California. She got in a day early and decided to visit the Sequoia and Kings Canyon National Parks less than an hour away. As she walked the trails of the parks marveling at the beauty of the massive trees, she thought back to her conversations with her friend and her pastor about forgiveness. As she strolled, Clara noticed that there were shadows everywhere from the towering canopy that blocked the full sunlight. The shadows dancing on the ground were a mirror image of the mental struggle in her mind. As she walked she prayed, telling God she knew she needed to forgive her father, but she didn't want to or much less know how. She felt the guilt her pastor and friend both placed on her and she asked God if he was angry with her for her weakness and disobedience in not forgiving. As soon as she asked God that question, she turned a corner and came to an opening. The sun burst through the opening above like streams of liquid silver. Little specks of gold floated through the light flickering like tiny fireflies. At once she was overwhelmed with the sense of God's love. She felt no anger, only unconditional love. It was on that path in the redwood forest that Clara came to the realization that forgiveness cannot be demanded but must be discovered. She prayed again for God to help her discover how to forgive. She ended her session by explaining that her journey toward forgiveness began in the redwood forest and ended the night after her mediation.

Clara's story is not unlike many other survivors of violent crimes. Another couple whose daughter was raped and murdered shared a similar experience. The couple was a part of a support group for families of murdered children. Shortly after their daughter's death, the pastor stopped by to visit and see how they were doing. In that meeting, the pastor explained even though it would be difficult they needed to forgive the man who killed their daughter. Both the mother and father explained they knew they should but felt if they forgave him they were in some way betraying their daughter. The pastor insisted it was important and urged them to pray with him to forgive. When they resisted the pastor became angry and explained if they didn't forgive they were choosing not to be forgiven of their sin and were in direct disobedience to God. The mother began to cry, explaining she just wasn't ready. The father was angry and asked the pastor to leave. That was the last time the couple had anything to do with the church they had attended for over twenty years. Clearly, Scripture does say to forgive so we can be forgiven. But nothing is ever gained by beating someone over the head with a Bible.

Misconceptions about Forgiveness

There are several misconceptions about forgiveness. The first is that if we forgive, we are letting the other person "off the hook." But forgiveness has nothing to do with justice. Clara forgave her father, but there was never any justice provided in that situation. He never admitted guilt and his death killed any possible opportunity for justice. The forgiveness that Clara finally offered her father happened in her own skin. Her father was no more off the hook after she forgave than he was before.

Another misconception about forgiveness is that people who forgive are weak. In our society, many people see forgiveness as a sign of weakness. In the highly competitive individualistic Western culture it is easier to judge and condemn our enemies than it is to empathize or forgive them. But the truth is forgiveness takes great strength as you will see in the next section.

Forgiveness is not about releasing the person who did the harm from responsibility. In restorative justice, that is quite the contrary. The ultimate goal would be for the one who did the harm to take responsibility for that and, in doing so, create the greatest possible scenario for them to receive forgiveness. Thomas's daughter forgave him for what he did to her. But Thomas continued to take full responsibility for his actions. Every offender who has participated in a victim-offender dialogue in prison and has received forgiveness goes right back to their cell afterward because they were responsible for the crime they committed. Forgiveness did not provide amnesty for the crime.

Forgiveness is not about trust or reconciliation. Remember the words of the young woman who met with the man who murdered her mother (see chapter 5), "I don't feel like I am talking to an enemy. I don't feel that I could ever have tea or nothing with you. But, like I said, I don't hate you at all." There was no reconciling that relationship nor would anyone expect there should be. A survivor of domestic violence can forgive the abuser, but trusting the abuser or attempting reconciliation would be dangerous.

A final misconception of forgiveness is that it is instant. For some people, as read earlier, it can be immediate. But, as we have seen with other stories of multiple survivors throughout this book, forgiveness takes time and considerable effort. One reason some people choose not to forgive is that it is not time to forgive. For some it is important to process the trauma and pain caused by another in order to truly determine what is being forgiven.

The Ultimate Story of Forgiveness

To understand the fullness of forgiveness, let's go to the story of ultimate forgiveness. Once again, let's go back to the beginning, the story of Abel whose blood cried out from the ground. It is Jesus who ultimately makes things right as seen later in the New Testament. "You have come to God, the Judge of all, to the spirits of the righteous made perfect, to Jesus the mediator of a new covenant, and to the sprinkled blood that speaks a better word than the blood of Abel" (Heb. 12:23–24). It is the sprinkled blood of Jesus that ushered in the new covenant. Jesus himself tells us at the Last Supper, "This is my blood of the covenant, which is poured out for many for the forgiveness of sins" (Matt. 26:28). The story of the cross is the ultimate story of forgiveness. Christ who knew no sin, took upon himself the sins of the world so we can receive forgiveness. He willingly chose to go to Calvary, though it was not an easy choice. It was in the garden where Christ "being in anguish, [he] prayed more earnestly, and his sweat was like drops of blood falling to the ground" (Luke 22:44). He said to his disciples, "'My soul is overwhelmed with sorrow to the point of death. Stay here and keep watch with me.' Going a little farther, he fell with his face to the ground and prayed, 'My Father, if it is possible, may this cup be taken from me. Yet not as I will, but as you will'" (Matt. 26:38–39). Forgiveness was not an easy task for Christ. In addition to causing him anguish, it caused him to sweat drops of blood and to be overwhelmed with sorrow. Nowhere in the story of the crucifixion do we see weakness. Forgiveness does not indicate weakness on the part of Christ; on the contrary, it reveals the ultimate strength.

What makes the Easter story powerful is the contrast between life and death. It is easy to celebrate the resurrection and new life. But that new life came at a cost. Resurrection life arose from the shadow of the cross. We must hold up the ugliness and sorrow and burden of the cross to Christ's resurrection. In doing that, the glorious light of new life takes on greater significance and radiates even brighter. Remember the words of the woman in the preface, "It was as if a boulder has been sitting on my chest for the last ten years, slowly crushing the breath out of me, crushing the life out of me, and now it's gone. Now, it's as if I can breathe again, live again." It took ten years of slowly dying before she found that place of new life.

If it was not easy for Christ to forgive, it is understandable how it can be difficult for us. Remember also, he was innocent but still chose to bear our sins. Clara was an innocent child, yet she was forced to bear the sin of her father. So much of Clara's story reflects the words of Christ where her soul was "overwhelmed with sorrow to the point of death." She didn't want to forgive but through great travail, she was able to follow in the footsteps of Jesus and forgive her father.

If you struggle to forgive someone who harmed you, fear not, you are not alone. You have permission to linger in the garden in anguish as you consider the overwhelming burden of forgiveness. You have permission to ask if there is any way you don't have to do it. It is with great hope you will eventually follow the steps of Christ, walk up your own dark hill where you too can whisper, "I forgive them, though they know not what they do." The cost is great but the reward is greater.

PART 3

The How

CHAPTER 9

Looking Ahead

When will I learn my lesson? I should know better by now. Clara beat herself up once again as she lay in the dark trying to sleep in a room full of other women, older women, snoring in the sleepful bliss Clara was not experiencing. Clara agreed to attend this prayer retreat for leaders of the organization Women Working for a Better Future, or WWBF. The nonprofit Clara ran was an affiliate of WWBF. Ever since the first retreat she attended the month before her mediation, Clara swore she would not put herself in that situation again. She was not a social person and hated being outside her comfort zone. But here she was, in a room full of twin beds wide awake and beating herself up for saying yes to join. A loud snort snapped her out of her thoughts. She realized there was no way she was going to be able to sleep with all the snoring women around her. With that, she grabbed her pillow and a blanket and went exploring for a quiet place to sleep. On the third floor of the country home housing the retreat she found a small room with a sign on the outside that read, "Prayer Closet."

Opening the door, Clara immediately sensed an overwhelming calm she hadn't felt since arriving earlier that morning. The velour recliner with gold and brown fall leaves and knobby wood sides, which looked like it stepped right out of the seventies, called her name. As she settled into the soft fabric she thought of her Nanna.

Nanna was her mother's mother and Clara loved when she was allowed to spend a week with her. Nanna had a velvety chair just like this one. Nanna's house—particularly Nanna's chair—was one of her favorite places in the world. That home was the safest place in the world. No monsters would creep down the halls at night. She would fall asleep each night listening to the stories of days gone by of antique dolls and lost treasures. She always felt love, real love, when she was with Nanna.

As she sat in the dark, she thought back to the day she met with Thomas. It was such a profound meeting. The relief she felt afterward was indescribable. It was as if she weighed twenty pounds lighter. She mentally walked through the mediation and remembered the picture she showed Thomas of her as a small child with dark sad eyes. As soon as the image of that small girl came to her mind, she was also hit with words, *It is time to let her go.* She was caught off guard by the words and knew instantly what God was saying. It was just a thought but Clara knew in her heart of hearts it was a message from God, a message that it was time to let go of the image and the reality of that sad little girl. Clara struggled with the concept. That little girl was in reality her inner identity. She said it often, she has always been sad. Even after the mediation with Thomas, she carried that sadness with her. The sadness was her comfort because it was familiar and the heaviness of the sorrow, while uncomfortable, at least told her she was alive. The idea of not having that sorrow in her life caught her off guard. She began to argue internally with God. *But she is all I know. What if I let go of the little girl, or in reality the sorrow and never have any intense feelings again? I would rather feel deep sorrow than nothing and live a mediocre life. God, I don't know great joy, only deep sorrow, I don't want to be left with nothing.*

Despite all her arguing and fretting, there was no answer. She knew God expected her to choose a different life. Immediately, the words of Moses found in Deuteronomy 30:19 came to mind: "I call heaven and earth as witnesses today against you, *that* I have set before you life and death, blessing and cursing; therefore choose life, that both you and your descendants may live" (NKJV). Clara knew God was giving her an ultimatum. She was to choose life or death. She was to choose to let go of the old that weighed her down to enter into a new unknown. Clara thought about the times she told friends that she actually died a long time ago, at the hands of her father, but her body hadn't figured it out. But this night God was challenging her to choose life. She knew she should but was not ready. After several hours of thinking and struggling, Clara finally fell asleep in the soft velvety chair. The next morning the first thought she had was about choosing life. She put it out of her mind and got up to begin the day. The next two days of the retreat were uneventful, other than the fact she kept thinking about the choice to be made.

She told the leader of the retreat that she was unable to sleep in the room with all the other women and preferred to sleep in the recliner on the third floor, which was fine. The last night of the retreat, the third night she had settled into that soft chair, she hoped to drift off quickly, but the nagging thought of the choice still hung heavy in her mind. Realizing God was not going to let her off the hook, she finally said out loud in the empty room, "Okay, God, have your way. I will choose life." There was no flash of light from heaven or chorus of angels singing in celebration, only silence. Clara didn't feel any different but at least now the nagging thoughts had stopped.

Clara returned home to her usual routine and eventually forgot about the time in the third-floor prayer closet. One afternoon she decided to take some time off and get some things done around the house. The last chore was pulling weeds out of the backyard garden. Afterward she sat on the tree swing her husband had built to enjoy the beautiful spring day. As she was swinging she was overwhelmed with a sense of joy at the beauty of both her surroundings and her life. The soft breeze and the vibrant yellow and orange Gerbera daisies were glorious. Her life was so amazing. Her children were getting ready to go off to college and they were happy, healthy, and eager to start a new phase. As Clara sat experiencing the bliss of her life, she remembered the night in the velvety chair. She felt nothing when she surrendered that day and chose life. She had no idea how God had moved her from that place of sorrow and death to this new life of hope and joy. Immediately the 23rd Psalm came to mind. She went inside, grabbed her Bible and her journal, and returned to the swing. She opened her journal and reread her personal version of Psalm 23. She chose life that night in the tiny room and God delivered. Tears flowed as she closed the book reflecting on the profound reality of the last lines. "How is it I fear no evil in these depths . . . because thy rod and thy staff, they comfort me." She was finally free, finally alive.

Next Steps

Clara's story is a beautiful example of how restorative justice processes can dramatically transform a survivor. Restorative justice worked for Clara as it has worked for thousands of others. So, the big question for you as the reader is, "Now what?"

The simple answer is found in restorative justice. But the path to get there may not be that simple. There are two phases organizations must go through to create a sacred space for survivors of sexual violence through restorative justice. Phase one involves examining the existing culture within your church, organization, or workplace. Phase two is implementing restorative justice concepts and processes. If the culture of your church, organization, or workplace is healthy and nurturing, then moving to phase two is all that is needed. If a toxic culture exists, it must be dismantled before implementing any restorative justice processes. But restorative justice concepts can also become the tools to dismantle toxicity. So, in reality, restorative justice is the thread woven throughout the process.

There are two parts to this chapter. The first part explores examining the existing culture within your organization, church, or workplace and dismantling existing toxic cultures, if necessary. The second part explores the steps necessary in order to implement restorative justice in your context.

Part 1: Examining and Dismantling

Every home, workplace, church, and organization has an existing culture. Existing cultures found within an organization include behaviors, norms, habits, rules—some hidden—and information. While many organizations are aware of and may even feel they have a good understanding of the organization's current culture, that does not mean the perceived desired culture actually exists. Think about it. We know toxic workplaces and organizations exist. Do you think the leadership of those entities knowingly implemented toxicity? Often, toxic cultures exist because someone in leadership is turning a blind eye to the actual reality. To ensure you are not that leader, it is important to explore and dive deep in assessing your existing culture.

There can be different levels of toxicity in cultures. In some cases, toxicity is so prevalent that it is evident to many in the organization and must be challenged. But the opposite can also exist; that toxicity is so entrenched, hidden, or dismissed that it is difficult to name. The second is particularly true where patriarchy exists. For the purposes of this book, patriarchy is defined as an organizational or social structure that is a male-dominated power structure where women in leadership is excluded or minimized. Typically, patriarchal organizations have historical roots and have existed so long that those in leadership are blind to their toxicities' existence. In those environments, you may hear things like "That's just the way things are" or "That's how we have always done things." Even if you think patriarchy is not an issue, don't dismiss the fact that there may be issues in your current churches, organizations, and businesses that demonstrate some toxicity regarding sexual violence.

If your church, organization, or workplace is serious about creating sacred space for survivors of sexual violence, the first step is to determine the existing culture in your organization. If patriarchy and toxicity exist, the critical question to ask is this: Is leadership aware of its existence? If the answer to that question is yes, unless that leadership has a "come to Jesus moment," much of what is in this section will be irrelevant and, in some situations, even dangerous to implement. But there is hope if leadership truly desires to eliminate patriarchy and toxicity. If patriarchy exists, power is an issue that must be acknowledged. Leadership in these types of structures must be willing to concede they don't know what they don't know and be ready to consider the potential harm that has existed.

The elements of restorative justice—direct voice, stakeholder focus, accountability, clarity around values, and a safe/structured environment—create the roadmap to identifying variables that need to be addressed. These include identifying bias, addressing microaggressions, exploring silence, evaluating personal and corporate accountability for harm, and examining policies and internal structures.

Direct Voice and Stakeholder Focus

Just like in restorative justice processes, the concept of direct voice can play a vital role in assessing culture. Ensure everyone within the organization has a voice in the process. The stakeholders must be identified. Churches could include pastors, staff, and congregants. In the workplace, all levels of employees and management are stakeholders. For organizations, stakeholders include management, staff, and clients. Once stakeholders are identified, leadership must communicate the desire to hear what others say about the organizational culture.

Applying direct voice doesn't necessarily mean every person in a particular culture must have a voice, although they could. But it could be that each level of management or subgroup within the culture can have a say in addressing problems. The opportunity should be open to all who want to speak into the process. Remember, those impacted negatively in toxic cultures may not be quick to speak up. This is where the other elements of restorative justice come into play.

Accountability

In this section, accountability refers to how the church, organization, or employer takes responsibility when harm occurs. If your church, organization, or business has never formally addressed how to take responsibility for harm, a starting place would be to inform members and employees of the desire to address accountability on all levels. The first step is to learn the ways we avoid accountability. Familiarize yourself with the thinking errors discussed in chapter 2.

One of the questions that must be included in assessing a toxic culture is, Has leadership ever created harmful situations or done harm that was never acknowledged or addressed? If you are the leader, begin with an internal self-reflection of how you would react if it is discovered that harm has occurred and was not acknowledged or addressed. Are you willing to concede responsibility for creating that harm? Are you ready to acknowledge and address it without employing the thinking errors? This is harder than you realize. Think about a time you do know you hurt someone else. Stop what you are doing right now, stop reading, and sit down and write a brief letter of apology to that person.

If you just did that activity, how easily were you tempted to justify, blame, or use any of the thinking errors? Understand that the same will occur when you learn that you have played a role in the existence of toxicity in your organization. Before providing stakeholders a direct voice in identifying harmful cultures, this must be considered. Leadership must be willing to hear of negative situations without adverse reactions or thinking errors. Without this level of accountability from leadership, the potential for ongoing harm is likely.

While it is unpleasant to acknowledge the harm we have done openly, it is the best starting point to dismantling a toxic culture. Not only that, but a wonderful by-product is modeling the behavior to others in the organization.

Clarifying Values

As mentioned in chapter 3, values tend to be the interests that motivate people to take positions on specific issues. Where there is a toxic culture, there will always be evidence of disparate values. Identifying the stakeholders' values will provide insight into what needs to be eliminated or changed to ensure a healthy environment. There are two levels of clarifying values of culture. The first is to identify the values individuals bring to the organization. The second is to determine what values are essential to the organization or workplace to create a healthy environment and succeed in accomplishing the organization's purpose.

Values can be identified through a variety of means. One method would be to create an anonymous poll for all stakeholders asking questions like, what values are important to you in general? What values do you bring to the table? What values are creating a challenging work/organizational environment? Another method would be to form groups to discuss and explore values stakeholders bring to the organization and values they see as essential to create a healthy, productive environment. Keep in mind, if any groups are formed they should consist of ethnic and gender equality. Also, if groups are created, it can be helpful to return to all stakeholders to ensure that the values identified by the group benefit everyone. It may also be beneficial to clarify to stakeholders that decisions will be made through consensus, meaning each person agrees to the values, even if it is not exactly what they expected initially. This decision reflects the understanding that individuals' values are important, but the overall work environment is also important.

Safe/Structured Environment

Beginning the work of identifying culture and, more importantly, dismantling a toxic culture, will be a challenge. Structure and thoughtfulness become the platform that allows stakeholders to engage safely. How each organization, church, or workplace will roll out this process will vary. But what is vital is that a method and structure be determined before doing any of the work in the previous sections on direct voice, stakeholder focus, accountability, and clarifying values. One option would be to create a small workgroup representative of all stakeholders. The goal of this group would be to determine how each phase of exploring existing culture and, if necessary, dismantling toxicity would happen.

Some groups may need to start by simply determining who the stakeholders are, asking whether they have considered all those impacted by their culture. It may be easy to see the internal stakeholders like employees or clients. But are other noninternal stakeholders such as customers, family members, or the community affected by the culture? Other groups may realize it is more important to begin with exploring values. What is important, no matter the starting point of the phases that follow, is to ensure that all the elements of restorative justice are in place.

Just as in chapter 4, it is critical to determine whether negative behaviors like fear, microaggressions, or unhealthy silence exist. These negative behaviors can be addressed and dismantled in the next section by creating healthy policies and structures that recognize the harmful repercussion of this behavior and implementing policies that clearly articulate they will no longer be tolerated. Equally important is to challenge stakeholders to consider personal biases and how those play a role in creating a healthier culture. It cannot be stated more emphatically that this element must be in place for any work to dismantle a toxic culture.

Policies and Structures

The last and very fundamental category is to examine existing policies and structures. Many organizations already have policies to address issues around sexual harassment and sexual violence. Suppose there are none in place; the first step is to write them. If there are existing policies, are all the elements addressed in this section included in the policies? Are there processes to address biases when they occur? Is there a policy about the use of microaggressions? Is there a process for individuals who don't speak up due to unhealthy reasons like power imbalances to have alternative communication methods? If the answer to each of these questions is no, and you are serious about making changes, writing policies is the first place to start. There are a variety of resources online to address policies around these issues. If you need legal advice upon which you intend to rely in your organization, church, or workplace, it may be necessary to consult a competent, independent attorney.

Policies alone cannot ensure an environment is not toxic or unhealthy. The structure within the organization is also important to consider. Denton Bible Church, mentioned in chapter 7, is a perfect example of an unhealthy church culture. First, there was no accountability by leadership early on. Fortunately, in the end, leadership assumed accountability, but so much damage was already done between the time that they should have and the time they did. In their letter to the congregation, the elders wrote, "Our church culture lacked involvement of women in decision-making processes related to the abuse of these girls. Further, in almost all meetings with the victims, no women were present, which was inappropriate."[1]

The lack of women involved is a structural issue. A quick look at the church's website reveals it is still the church's culture. Only 18 percent of the staff or leadership are women. Of the women listed, 70 percent are in roles that are gender traditional, like girl's or women's ministries. It is the hope that leadership knows the error of not including women in decision-making processes, and that those demographics will be different in the future.

There is nothing worse than asking people for their opinion about issues and then just letting the gathered material collect dust on the shelf. On par with that is giving lip service by implementing suggested changes but never providing any follow-up to ensure changes were made or to enforce those changes. So, once changes are identified and implemented, create periodic check-ins and evaluations to ensure things are working and change has occurred.

Finally, it is important to state that toxic cultures can be like cockroaches. They may seem to disappear, but often they are behind walls or in cracks waiting to reemerge. It would be naive for any organization to do a walk through and make changes and think that is all that must be done. That is the starting point. It also takes intentionality to ensure all stakeholders maintain changes implemented. Change is hard and human nature is to go back to what is comfortable. Transformation does not occur in a linear fashion. Yes, you can put steps in place like details in this section and they may function in a linear way. But transformation is also cyclical. Anytime transformation or change is implemented, most people or organizations will cycle in and out of the positive new expectations and the negative old ways of doing things. How many people make New Year's resolutions and within a few short weeks find old habits creeping back in? It is simply human nature. The same will happen when trying to change negative toxic culture. Don't freak out when the cockroaches of the past crawl back out. Just do what needs to be done and address them. It's not so important that negative ways of doing things emerge again, what is important is how often they emerge, how significant the harms, and how efficient the response will be to ensure the frequency continues to diminish until the new, healthy culture is so enmeshed that it is permanent.

So, once policies and processes are identified and changed to create a healthier culture, set up quarterly check-ins to see where old habits are trying to resurface. The structure of monitoring can help maintain the safe/structured environment for everyone involved.

Part 2: Implementing

Only after the culture has been evaluated and, if necessary, changes implemented would your organization move to the next step to determine how to create a sacred space for survivors of sexual violence. If you used the elements of restorative justice to assess your organization's culture, you are already on your way to becoming a restorative organization, even if you never actually implement restorative justice processes. To take that even further, the questions below can help determine a few ideas for creating a more restorative culture. The elements of restorative justice can be woven throughout any existing structure creating restorative practices and culture. The possibilities are endless.

Where can direct voice be implemented?

Whose voice is not at the table?

How can our organization hear more directly and specifically from all members?

Where is accountability expected when harm happens?

How is accountability being modeled?

What are opportunities to increase repairing harm and making things right?

What areas can benefit from increasing all levels of leadership in the process or dialogue?

Who in our organization is historically omitted from programming?

Is there a structure in place that allows members to feel safe and speak out?

Do all members feel respected?

Does our organization create opportunities for individuals to choose to engage or not?

Do we know the values of all our members?

Are there processes or opportunities in place to address differing values?

For organizations, churches, or businesses that want to go further and implement restorative justice processes like circles, family group conferences, or victim-offender dialogue, the commitment toward survivors' well-being must be front and center. This commitment will then inform the organizational processes that need to be developed. The organizational strategies should include fo-

cus areas, necessary partnerships, program development, training, policies and procedures, and restorative justice philosophy
and process communication.

Focus Areas

The first organizational strategy is to create and implement processes and programs for survivors of sexual violence. Before
identifying a program or methodology, it is necessary to determine the focus. The focus will drive program development and
all other phases of implementation. One focus could be creating
processes to address sexual harm or violence within the existing
organization. In that case, program development would include
training facilitators and implementing restorative justice processes like circles, family group conferences, or victim-offender
dialogue. Policies and procedures would focus on accountability
and repairing harm. Another focus could be to create spaces for
healing for survivors of sexual violence. This may take the form of
creating a support system for survivors, including counseling, support groups, and healing circles. The program development and
partnerships would differ significantly from the previous focus.

There are two scenarios for determining focus. The first scenario is reactive in that sexual violence has occurred within the organization, and leaders and stakeholders are demanding change.
This scenario may require a more robust implementation of all the
restorative justice principles and processes. The second scenario
is proactive, where the organization, church, or workplace has not
yet had issues arise, but wants to act to ensure they never do. No
matter the scenario or desired goals, considering the focus is the
starting place.

One last consideration regarding focus is the scope. Is the goal
to provide support and internal processes within the existing en-

tity, or will the focus include internal and external survivors of sexual violence? This form of focus will determine not only program development but also potential partnerships.

Potential Partnerships

Providing and meeting the needs of sexual survivors will require partnerships on some level. What role will law enforcement play in the program development? In the case of an outcry of sexual violence against a child, mandatory reporting must be done. A healthy relationship with reporting agencies will benefit all parties, including the victim. But there may be cases of reported sexual violence in your context where law enforcement is unnecessary. Remember the statistics in the introduction: only 23 percent of victims of sexual assault or rape reported the crime to the police.

Either way, it may be beneficial to explore your community's legal system. Reach out to the local police, district attorney, victim advocates, and courts and learn all you can about what currently exists in your community to support survivors. Learn what services are provided and explore those entities' mindsets or philosophies. Are they open to a restorative approach, or are they more traditional in approaching sexual violence and crimes? The more aligned your organization is with the vision and goals of a potential partner, the more effective the relationship will be. This does not mean you cannot partner with groups that do not share a restorative justice philosophy, but be mindful of how that lack of shared vision will impact the work.

Sadly, many churches, nonprofits, and other organizations operate in a solo mindset of providing services with little collaboration with other groups. When this happens, everyone loses. So once the focus is determined, ask and explore who are potential partners and how to engage those partnerships.

Program Development

Program development is the most time-consuming phase of implementing restorative justice processes in your context. This phase must include significant exploration into existing services and programs within the community. And remember, the heart of any program development is the commitment to the survivor's well-being. Stakeholder focus is needed in program development. Sexual violence involves and impacts multiple stakeholders, including the victim, the offender, law enforcement, families, and the community. Sexual violence affects communities, so community representation is necessary for program development. There is a plethora of resources on program development. Do your research. Seek out existing organizations, churches, and businesses that already provide restorative justice processes and learn from them. Every state has programs and services for survivors. Seek them out and ask to learn more about the procedures and policies they use to provide their program support. Remember, there is no need to reinvent the wheel. But it is important to determine best practices and look for programs with a healthy track record of supporting, healing, repairing, and expecting accountability from those who have done harm. One organization took the policies and procedures used by the state-funded victim-offender dialogue and modified them to meet their need to provide reconciliation circles where harm had been done internally. Providing a step-by-step plan for program development in this section is impossible because each entity has different goals and expectations. But a good starting place would be to create a workgroup representative of stakeholders to explore program development. Be willing to include individuals outside your organization, church, or workplace. Consider potential members that include victims, members of the criminal justice system, law enforcement, counselors, families, nonprofit organizations, schools, indigenous communities, and businesses. Some representation from the legal field, either law enforcement or an attorney, can be helpful to ensure any new programs remain within what is legally acceptable. But if outside members are included, they must understand the expectations and philosophy of implementing restorative justice programming in your context.

Training

Training is an absolute must for any group considering creating sacred space for survivors of sexual violence. Typically, most courses offered are between thirty and forty hours. These courses may be offered by groups like Dispute Resolution Centers or any group that trains some forms of mediators. Look for training opportunities that address the following topics:

- philosophy and principles of restorative justice
- skills including facilitation skills, skills to recognize and address the abuse of power, and other skills necessary for working with victims, offenders, and other stakeholders
- victim sensitivity
- trauma and its impact
- interests of participants
- process guidelines and expectations
- accountability and thinking errors

Policies and Procedures

Policies and procedures need to be developed and followed before implementing any services. Remember, the structure provided by implementing policies and procedures can create a safe/structured environment. Details that need to be included consist of the following:

- **Goals.** What are the goals for the program developed? For example, if a victim-offender program is being designed, goals may include: the opportunity for victims to meet with their offender in a safe/structured environment, to directly and constructively express to offender(s) thoughts and feelings around the crime, and to ask questions and receive answers and insight, which only the offender can provide.
- **Intake.** How will participants be onboarded into the programs? Most programs are victim initiated and voluntary. Reaching out to victims of sexual violence unsolicited is potentially harmful because there is no way to know where victims are in the aftermath of sexual violence. Receiving unsolicited contact concerning the crime could be a trigger for some victims. A "knock-on-the-door" approach, asking a victim if they would like to meet face-to-face with their offender, could be traumatizing. But, not reaching out to specific survivors creates a question of how to let survivors know that a program or process is available to them if they so choose. This is where potential partnerships can play a role. Victim advocates, counselors, law enforcement, and court personnel all have access to victims. They can inform them of potential programs like victim-offender dialogue or circles if and when they are interested and ready. A victim-initiated approach provides the most autonomy for survivors of sexual violence to determine the best path forward.
- **Preparation.** How do other programs prepare participants? A great way to determine how to prepare participants is by looking at other programs that provide restorative justice programming. Most states have some form of victim-offender

dialogue. Reach out to those programs and learn how they prepare their participants. Be careful from whom you seek information. Not every program using the term *restorative justice* will fall within the true principles and philosophy of proper restorative justice. One community had a program that provided spiritual support for offenders in prison and considered itself to be a restorative justice ministry because the work they were doing was restorative. But in reality, some critical elements of restorative justice were missing when one looked a little deeper into their program. The only stakeholder involved was the offender, and accountability was not required. Volunteers in the program could not even ask offenders about their crimes, allowing no means for or expectation to challenge the offender to take responsibility for their actions. For the most part, state-sanctioned restorative-justice programs are a safe resource starting point. Details to consider for preparation should include the following:

- How much time is involved in preparation?
- What tools will be provided to participants to prepare? Some examples are personal assessments of the impact of the crime, letters to the other participants, support systems, and interaction and assessment with a facilitator.

- **Confidentiality.** Most facilitated dialogue operates within the expectation of confidentiality. The sensitive nature of issues around sexual violence and trauma dictates the need for confidentiality. Again, look into other programming to see how confidentiality is addressed.
- **Monitoring.** Does the developing program require some level of monitoring? A situation where monitoring would be necessary is when repairing the harm is a part of the process. Harm can be repaired in a million ways and would be as individual as

each person in the process. An example could be that a survivor of workplace harassment may ask that classes be required to detail what is considered harassment and harmful. In this situation, some level of monitoring would need to exist to ensure what was agreed upon becomes a reality. In determining how to monitor, some issues to consider are

- the persons who will be monitoring,
- the timeline for completion of any agreements or resolutions made, and
- recourse for failing to meet goals.

- **Communication.** Once programs are developed, the next step is letting people know what is available. Communication delivered within the organization or to the community should clearly state the commitment to the well-being of survivors of sexual violence and the victim/survivor focus. While those who do the harm are involved in the process, language like "second chances" or "learning from mistakes" can undermine the victim-initiated focus of restorative justice. A safe way to help craft communication is to assume a survivor of sexual violence is listening to what is being communicated. Or even better, have a survivor help craft the communication. This will help ensure that the language falls on the ears of those you seek to help and for whom you hope to provide sacred space.

Processes to Consider

There are a variety of restorative justice processes that can be implemented. Organizations, churches, or workplaces must determine the appropriate process to achieve desired goals. Three processes to consider are circles, one-on-one dialogue, and surrogate dialogue.

Circles

Circles are a powerful tool used to address healing for survivors. The beauty of circles is found in the structure that doesn't vary while topics and dialogue within the process change all the time. The purpose of the circle can be almost anything. There can be outcome-based circles where a decision needs to be made, for example, when harm is done. The circle can be the process for participants to understand the full impact of the harm and decide what needs to be done to make things right. There are circles for healing, circles for celebrating, and circles for understanding. Circles can be the process used for strategic planning on implementing concepts in this book. There is no limit to the topics that can be addressed in a circle.

Your organization may use circles in which the participants are survivors in an effort to provide support and healing for them. That support circle could be broadened to include other stakeholders who are able to provide support and healing to survivors. Circles to create understanding can help others in your organization understand the trauma and challenges facing survivors of sexual violence. And finally, a circle for celebration can be a wonderful process to celebrate all the hard work done to make a difference in the lives of survivors.

One-on-One Dialogue

Most organizations won't need to create programs like victim-offender dialogue since those need to occur within the criminal justice system. But the same concept can be used for other conflicts and harm within a church, an organization, or a workplace. In the context of sexual misconduct, this one-on-one process can be more comfortable than circles. Some individuals who have experienced sexual harassment or misconduct would feel very uncomfortable addressing the harm with a group of people, even if it is in a circle. Providing the opportunity for those harmed to meet one-on-one with the person who did the harm can benefit all involved. Of course, one-on-one meetings around the issue of sexual harm should always include a facilitator who will ensure the process is as safe as possible. The facilitator serves multiple purposes: to help with thinking errors, to watch and address power imbalances, and to help the participants determine what needs to happen to make things right. That last phrase is important: the participants determine the next steps, not the facilitator.

If the organization does not have someone internally who understands the concepts of restorative justice, the first step would be to identify resources and individuals that can help create healthy, safe processes. Outside training and resources are vital to ensure the concepts, methods, and policies follow best practices for restorative justice. Anyone facilitating circles or one-on-one dialogue would need outside training. Resources are available in every state for learning more about restorative justice, mediation, and mediated dialogue. Some agencies or organizations provide training for individuals interested in becoming restorative justice facilitators—look for groups that specifically offer training in restorative justice. Many states also have agencies or organizations that train laypeople in mediation.

Surrogate Dialogue

As seen in the story of Clara and Thomas, the surrogate process can be profoundly healing. If we know these dialogues work, what might they look like in other contexts? Shortly after the riots in Charlottesville, Virginia, in 2017, a handful of colleagues gathered to discuss how the event impacted them and their communities. A woman we will call Betty was experienced in restorative justice mediation and was a part of that group. She shared about surrogate mediation or circles and asked if there was a way to do something similar in this context. In this context, the surrogate offender would be Betty. Betty's family history included her father's great-grandfather, who was an officer in the Confederacy in the Civil War. Her father's uncle had participated in a lynching of a young Black man who was arrested for talking to a White girl in the early '60s.

Betty asked the group if there would be any value in doing a surrogate mediation with her and several of her family members who were ashamed of their history with African Americans who had felt the burden of racial inequality for years. The group readily agreed, and a meeting was scheduled. The circle consisted of six Black men and women and six White men and women, including Betty, her aunt, and one cousin. The rounds of the circle consisted of sharing the impact of racial trauma in the South that each person experienced. Of course, those who were White did not suffer because of the color of their skin. As Betty listened to the stories of loved ones persecuted or beaten simply because they were Black, her shame deepened. She represented the people who perpetuated that hate. Maybe she didn't hate as they did, but her people did significant harm in the past. During one of the rounds Betty's aunt broke down and expressed deep shame for what her family represented. She went on to say how remorseful she felt and wished there was something to do to make things right.

As the talking piece was passed to an older Black woman, the woman looked directly at Betty's aunt and said, "You can't make things right, honey. I wish you could. But what you did just now is exactly what this older woman needed. I needed to hear those words come out of your mouth."

The circle closed with tears of sorrow and thankfulness at the sacred moment they all experienced.

155

Processes like that circle can be used with survivors who want to experience what Betty and Clara did with surrogate dialogue, one-on-one or in a circle context. The context would determine the participants. Pastors, leaders, supervisors, and managers willing to step into the shoes of colleagues that harmed others and take responsibility for the people group they represent can provide accountability on some level for the harm done by their peers.

Final Thoughts

If we want to usher in justice, it is time to dismantle toxic environments and implement opportunities for healing. God clearly demands we do so. What we are seeing in our churches and society is not new. Read the words of Ezekiel:

> Behold, the rulers of Israel, each according to his power, have been among you for the purpose of shedding blood. They have treated father and mother with contempt among you. They have oppressed the stranger in your midst; they have oppressed the orphan and the widow among you. You have despised My holy things and profaned My Sabbaths. Slanderous men have been among you for the purpose of shedding blood, and among you they have eaten at the mountain shrines. In your midst they have committed outrageous sin. Among you, they have uncovered their fathers' nakedness; among you they have abused her who was unclean in her menstruation. And one has committed abomination with his neighbor's wife, another has outrageously defiled his daughter-in-law, and another among you has sexually abused his sister, his father's daughter. (Ezek. 22:6–11 NASB)

And the word of the Lord came to me, saying, "Son of man, say to her, 'You are a land that is not clean or rained on in the day of indignation.' There is a conspiracy of her prophets in her midst like a roaring lion tearing the prey. They have devoured lives; they have taken treasure and precious things; they have made many widows in the midst of her." (Ezek. 22:23–25 NASB)

These were the leaders of Israel. These were God's people. What is happening now has happened before over and over. But, we know God had other plans. Plans similar to what Thomas did as a surrogate. Ezekiel says, "I searched for a man among them who would build up a wall and stand in the gap before Me for the land, so that I would not destroy it; but I found no one" (22:30 NASB). God was looking for someone to stand in the gap. God was telling the Israelites then and he is telling us now, "It is time to step up and acknowledge our sins, our toxic silence, and our ability to harm. It is time for the brave to step into the shoes of those who refuse accountability and provide healing to survivors of sexual violence." How wonderful would it be if we could be wall builders like the people in Nehemiah, to be "found out that [I] had finished rebuilding the wall and that no gaps remained ..." (Neh. 6:1 NLT).

Survivors have demonstrated bravery we can all learn from and model. They are the bravest people on the planet. To rise from the ashes and devastation of sexual violence is nothing short of gargantuan courage. It is time to provide a place for survivors to sit in peace and rest from the daily struggle of living in the aftermath of violence. In providing space for healing and hope, and maybe, just maybe, there will be other Claras who can write, "How is it I fear no evil in these depths ... because thy rod and thy staff, they comfort me."

QUESTIONS TO CONSIDER

Chapter 1

1. Where could restorative justice be most valuable in your church, organization, or everyday life?
2. How does your church or organization provide opportunities to hear all voices within, even those with differing views?
3. Whose voice is not being heard or validated in your church or organization?
4. What problems seem to surface the most within your church or organization?
5. Could restorative justice be a resource for those problems?
6. If so, what could be some possible next steps?

Chapter 2

1. As a leader, do you model accountability when you make mistakes?
2. How does your church or organization address wrongs that occur?
3. How does your church or organization address conflict that arises?

4. What thinking errors come up most often in your interactions with your family, church, or organization?
5. Who needs to hear you say, "I was wrong; I know I hurt you. Can we talk?"

Chapter 3

1. How does your church or organization support those struggling with mental health issues?
2. Has denial been an issue in your church or organization?
3. Where have issues around sexual violence been evident in your church or organization?
4. Has denial played a role in the areas where there have been issues of sexual violence in your church or organization?
5. Has denial played a role in the areas with any of the stakeholders affected by the issues of sexual violence in your church or organization?
6. Does your church or organization attempt to engage all stakeholders when an issue arises, or are most conflicts handled by leadership or management?

Chapter 4

1. Where is binary thinking evident in my church or organization?
2. What are some examples of cognitive dissonance I have experienced?
3. How well does my church or organization deal with ambivalence?
4. In what areas have I demonstrated active listening?
5. What areas do I need to improve with active listening?

6. What role has preparation provided when conflict arises in my church or organization?

Chapter 5

1. What elements of safe place exist in your church or organization?
2. What programs might be a good fit for your church or organization?
3. Does your church or organization have policies and processes for addressing reports of sexual assault or harassment?
4. What is your personal opinion of #metoo and the #churchtoo movements?
5. How have you supported any friends and family who have identified as survivors of sexual violence?

Chapter 6

1. What examples of rape culture have you witnessed or heard?
2. What negative words appear most often in your church or organization?
3. Can you think of examples of questions you have asked that prompted an adverse reaction you didn't intend?
4. Can you think of examples of negative questions you were asked that prompted an adverse reaction in you or caused you to be caught off guard?
5. What personal biases would be challenging for you to suspend judgment temporarily?

Chapter 7

1. How are those in power held accountable in your church or organization?
2. Are there policies in place in your church or organization to address sexual violence?
3. Have you ever been impacted negatively by an imbalance of power? If yes, what emotions did you experience?
4. Have you ever experienced powerlessness? If yes, what emotions did you experience?

Chapter 8

1. What has been your practice in forgiving?
2. Have you ever struggled to forgive someone? If so, what made it challenging to do so?
3. Have you ever sought forgiveness and not received it? If so, how did you react and feel?
4. What thoughts on forgiveness in this chapter challenge you the most?

NOTES

Introduction

1. "Victims of Sexual Violence: Statistics," RAINN, https://www.rainn
.org/statistics/victims-sexual-violence.

2. Rachel E. Morgan and Grace Kena, "Criminal Victimization, 2016:
Revised," U.S. Department of Justice, Office of Justice Programs, *Bureau
of Justice Statistics*, https://bjs.ojp.gov/content/pub/pdf/cv16.pdf.

3. "Statistics About Sexual Violence," National Sexual Violence Resource Center, Info and Stats for Journalists, https://www.nsvrc.org
/sites/default/files/publications_nsvrc_factsheet_media-packet_statistics
-about-sexual-violence_0.pdf, 2.

4. "Responding to Transgender Victims of Sexual Assault," Office for
Victims of Crime, June 2014, https://ovc.ojp.gov/sites/g/files/xyckuh226
/files/pubs/forge/sexual_numbers.html.

5. "A Survey of LGBT Americans Chapter 6: Religion," Pew Research
Center, June 13, 2013, https://www.pewresearch.org/social-trends/2013
/06/13/chapter-6-religion/.

6. https://h-e-a-r-t.org.

7. Debbie Smith, "Victim vs. Survivor," February 5, 2023, https://h-e
-a-r-t.org/2023/02/victim-vs-survivor/.

Chapter 1

1. "Restorative Justice: A Framework for Fresno," https://www.iirp
.edu/images/pdf/bc04_fresno.pdf.

2. *Handbook on Restorative Justice Programmes*, Criminal Justice Handbook Series (New York: United Nations, 2006), 8, https://www.unodc.org

/pdf/criminal_justice/Handbook_on_Restorative_Justice_Programmes
.pdf.

3. Howard Zehr, *The Little Book of Restorative Justice*, 2nd ed. (New York: Good Books, 2015), 13.

Chapter 3

1. Justin Mitchell, "She Was Raped on a Popular Bridge Used for Exercise. Social Media Blamed Her for Walking Alone," *Clarion Ledger*, November 16, 2018. https://www.clarionledger.com/story/news/2018 /11/16/supporters-victim-blaming-woman-raped-ms-coast-bridge /1998538002/.

Chapter 4

1. "I, Too, Am Harvard," https://itooamharvard.tumblr.com/.

Chapter 5

1. "Victims of Sexual Violence: Statistics: Sexual Violence Can Have Long-Term Effects on Victims," RAINN, https://www.rainn.org/statistics /victims-sexual-violence.

2. These statistics come from studies gathered by RAIIN. See "Victims of Sexual Violence."

3. Barbara Olasov Rothbaum, Edna B. Foa, David S. Riggs, Tamera Murdock, and William Walsh, "A Prospective Examination of Post-Traumatic Stress Disorder in Rape Victims," *Journal of Traumatic Stress*, 5/3 (1992): 455–75.

4. Jonathan R. T. Davidson and Edna B. Foa, eds., *Posttraumatic Stress Disorder: DSM-IV and Beyond* (Washington, DC: American Psychiatric Press, 1992), 23–36.

5. Dean G. Kilpatrick, Christine M. Edmunds, and Anne Seymour, *Rape in America: A Report to the Nation*, a report published by the National Victim Center and Crime Victims Research and Treatment Center, April 23, 1992.

6. Lynn Langton and Jennifer L. Truman, "Socio-emotional Impact of Violent Crime," Department of Justice, Office of Justice Programs,

Bureau of Justice Statistics, September 2014, https://bjs.ojp.gov/content
/pub/pdf/sivc.pdf.

7. Office for Victims of Crime, "Victim Impact: Listen and Learn—
Debbie's Story," June 11, 2018, YouTube video, 5:10, https://youtu.be
/BHomtooO4uo?si=easvNhsfv_gvcGKM.

8. *Merriam-Webster's Collegiate Dictionary*, https://www.merriam
-webster.com/dictionary/ambivalence.

9. *Merriam-Webster's Collegiate Dictionary*, https://www.merriam
-webster.com/dictionary/cognitive%20dissonance.

10. Juliespeerproduction, "Sandy's Story & Restorative Mediation,"
April 12, 2011, YouTube video, 6:59, https://www.youtube.com/watch?v=
IJf_I4_8Ex4.

11. *Beyond Conviction*, directed by Rachel Libert, produced by Rachel
Libert, Jedd Wider, and Todd Wider (n.p.: CustomFlix, 2006), DVD, 97
min.

Chapter 6

1. Maria Popova, "'Sometimes': Poet and Philosopher David Whyte's
Stunning Meditation on Walking in the Questions of Our Becoming," *The
Marginalian*, August 19, 2020, https://www.themarginalian.org/2020/08
/19/david-whyte-sometimes/.

Chapter 7

1. "Congregational Update from the Denton Bible Church Elder
Board," Denton Bible Church (Denton, TX) congregational letter, May 1,
2022, https://www.scribd.com/document/598704928/Denton-Bible
-Church-Congregational-Letter-May-1-22#.

2. "Congregational Update"

Chapter 8

1. Everett L. Worthington Jr., PhD, Department of Psychology, Virginia Commonwealth University, April 2020, https://www.templeton.org
/wp-content/uploads/2020/06/Forgiveness_final.pdf. See p. 4.

2. Kirsten Weir, "Forgiveness Can Improve Mental and Physical

Health," American Psychological Association, CE Corner, January 2017, https://www.apa.org/monitor/2017/01/ce-corner.

3. Weir, "Forgiveness Can Improve Mental Health." For Toussaint's study see Loren L. Toussaint, Grant S. Shields, and George M. Slavich, "Forgiveness, Stress, and Health: A 5-Week Dynamic Parallel Process Study," National Library of Medicine, National Center for Biotechnology Information, Annals of Behavioral Medicine, October 2016, https://pubmed.ncbi.nlm.nih.gov/27068160/.

4. Kerri O'Brien, "'I Am Finally Free': Virginia Rape Victim and DNA Evidence Advocate Confronts Her Attacker," WRIC ABC8News, November 9, 2021, https://www.wric.com/news/taking-action/i-am-finally-free-virginia-rape-victim-and-dna-advocate-confronts-her-attacker/.

5. O'Brien, "'I Am Finally Free.'"

Chapter 9

1. Leonardo Blair, "Texas Megachurch Repents for Not Involving Women in Decision-Making after Abuse of 14 Girls by Ex-pastor," The Christian Post, October 5, 2022, https://www.christianpost.com/news/texas-megachurch-repents-for-no-women-in-decision-making.html.